The Tragedie of
Julius Caesar

By Edward de Vere

Art:
Portrait of Edward de Vere
17th Earl of Oxford (1550-1604)

This edition produced by
Verus Publishing

V | P

www.verusbooks.com

ISBN: 978-1-951267-39-1
Imprint / Publisher: Verus Publishing

The Author

Edward de Vere, 17th Earl of Oxford

Biography and Bibliography
After the Play

A Preverse

Drone on ye learned scholars of the day
As to with whom the words ahead the credit lay.
For our part though can be no further doubt
That the author of these words has been found out
To be a person lordly and refined
On whom the light of wit so boldly shined
That to keep this wit from tearing in the fray
He gave another, lesser wit his say.

Now let the least of wits
That writes these paltry lines
Yield to him whose peerless name
Should be with reverence spake.
Let this name be not of history's misassigns
Whose pen and verse have made the earth to shake.

The Tragedie of
Julius Caesar

By Edward de Vere

The Main Characters

Julius Caesar

Triumvirs after Caesar's Death

Octavius Caesar
Mark Antony
Lepidus

The Conspirators against Caesar

Marcus Brutus (Brutus)
Cassius
Casca
Decius Brutus
Cinna
Metellus Cimber
Trebonius

Caius Ligarius

Tribunes

Flavius
Marullus

Roman Senators

Cicero
Publius
Popilius Lena

Citizens

Calpurnia – Wife of Caesar
Portia – Wife of Brutus
A Soothsayer
Artemidorus – A Sophist from Knidos
Cinna – A poet
Cobbler
Carpenter
Poet
Lucius – Attendant to Brutus

Loyal to Brutus and Cassius

Volumnius
Titinius
Young Cato – Brother of Portia
Messala – A messenger

Varrus
Clitus
Claudio
Dardanius
Strato
Pindarus – Cassius' bondman

And now, the Play...

ACT I

SCENE I.

Rome. A street.

Enter FLAVIUS, MARULLUS, and certain Commoners

FLAVIUS
Hence! home, you idle creatures get you home:
Is this a holiday? what! know you not,
Being mechanical, you ought not walk
Upon a labouring day without the sign
Of your profession? Speak, what trade art thou?
First Commoner
Why, sir, a carpenter.
MARULLUS
Where is thy leather apron and thy rule?
What dost thou with thy best apparel on?
You, sir, what trade are you?
Second Commoner
Truly, sir, in respect of a fine workman, I am but,
as you would say, a cobbler.
MARULLUS
But what trade art thou? answer me directly.
Second Commoner
A trade, sir, that, I hope, I may use with a safe
conscience; which is, indeed, sir, a mender of bad soles.
MARULLUS
What trade, thou knave? thou naughty knave, what
trade?
Second Commoner
Nay, I beseech you, sir, be not out with me: yet,
if you be out, sir, I can mend you.
MARULLUS

What meanest thou by that? mend me, thou saucy
fellow!
Second Commoner
Why, sir, cobble you.
FLAVIUS
Thou art a cobbler, art thou?
Second Commoner
Truly, sir, all that I live by is with the awl: I
meddle with no tradesman's matters, nor women's
matters, but with awl. I am, indeed, sir, a surgeon
to old shoes; when they are in great danger, I
recover them. As proper men as ever trod upon
neat's leather have gone upon my handiwork.
FLAVIUS
But wherefore art not in thy shop today?
Why dost thou lead these men about the streets?
Second Commoner
Truly, sir, to wear out their shoes, to get myself
into more work. But, indeed, sir, we make holiday,
to see Caesar and to rejoice in his triumph.
MARULLUS
Wherefore rejoice? What conquest brings he home?
What tributaries follow him to Rome,
To grace in captive bonds his chariot-wheels?
You blocks, you stones, you worse than senseless
things!
O you hard hearts, you cruel men of Rome,
Knew you not Pompey? Many a time and oft
Have you climb'd up to walls and battlements,
To towers and windows, yea, to chimney-tops,
Your infants in your arms, and there have sat
The livelong day, with patient expectation,
To see great Pompey pass the streets of Rome:
And when you saw his chariot but appear,

Have you not made an universal shout,
That Tiber trembled underneath her banks,
To hear the replication of your sounds
Made in her concave shores?
And do you now put on your best attire?
And do you now cull out a holiday?
And do you now strew flowers in his way
That comes in triumph over Pompey's blood? Be gone!
Run to your houses, fall upon your knees,
Pray to the gods to intermit the plague
That needs must light on this ingratitude.
FLAVIUS
Go, go, good countrymen, and, for this fault,
Assemble all the poor men of your sort;
Draw them to Tiber banks, and weep your tears
Into the channel, till the lowest stream
Do kiss the most exalted shores of all.

Exeunt all the Commoners

See whether their basest metal be not moved;
They vanish tongue-tied in their guiltiness.
Go you down that way towards the Capitol;
This way will I
disrobe the images,
If you do find them deck'd with ceremonies.
MARULLUS
May we do so?
You know it is the feast of Lupercal.
FLAVIUS
It is no matter; let no images
Be hung with Caesar's trophies. I'll about,
And drive away the vulgar from the streets:
So do you too, where you perceive them thick.
These growing feathers pluck'd from Caesar's wing

Will make him fly an ordinary pitch,
Who else would soar above the view of men
And keep us all in servile fearfulness.

Exeunt

SCENE II.

A public place.

*Flourish. Enter CAESAR; ANTONY, for the course;
CALPURNIA, PORTIA, DECIUS BRUTUS, CICERO,
BRUTUS, CASSIUS, and CASCA; a great crowd following,
among them a Soothsayer*

CAESAR
Calpurnia!
CASCA
Peace, ho! Caesar speaks.
CAESAR
Calpurnia!
CALPURNIA
Here, my lord.
CAESAR
Stand you directly in Antonius' way,
When he doth run his course. Antonius!
ANTONY
Caesar, my lord?
CAESAR
Forget not, in your speed, Antonius,
To touch Calpurnia; for our elders say,
The barren, touched in this holy chase,
Shake off their sterile curse.
ANTONY
I shall remember:
When Caesar says 'do this,' it is perform'd.

CAESAR
Set on; and leave no ceremony out.

Flourish

Soothsayer
Caesar!
CAESAR
Ha! who calls?
CASCA
Bid every noise be still: peace yet again!
CAESAR
Who is it in the press that calls on me?
I hear a tongue, shriller than all the music,
Cry 'Caesar!' Speak; Caesar is turn'd to hear.
Soothsayer
Beware the ides of March.
CAESAR
What man is that?
BRUTUS
A soothsayer bids you beware the ides of March.
CAESAR
Set him before me; let me see his face.
CASSIUS
Fellow, come from the throng; look upon Caesar.
CAESAR
What say'st thou to me now? speak once again.
Soothsayer
Beware the ides of March.
CAESAR
He is a dreamer; let us leave him: pass.

Sennet. Exeunt all except BRUTUS and CASSIUS

CASSIUS

Will you go see the order of the course?
BRUTUS
Not I.
CASSIUS
I pray you, do.
BRUTUS
I am not gamesome: I do lack some part
Of that quick spirit that is in Antony.
Let me not hinder, Cassius, your desires;
I'll leave you.
CASSIUS
Brutus, I do observe you now of late:
I have not from your eyes that gentleness
And show of love as I was wont to have:
You bear too stubborn and too strange a hand
Over your friend that loves you.
BRUTUS
Cassius,
Be not deceived: if I have veil'd my look,
I turn the trouble of my countenance
Merely upon myself. Vexed I am
Of late with passions of some difference,
Conceptions only proper to myself,
Which give some soil perhaps to my behaviors;
But let not therefore my good friends be grieved--
Among which number, Cassius, be you one--
Nor construe any further my neglect,
Than that poor Brutus, with himself at war,
Forgets the shows of love to other men.
CASSIUS
Then, Brutus, I have much mistook your passion;
By means whereof this breast of mine hath buried
Thoughts of great value, worthy cogitations.
Tell me, good Brutus, can you see your face?

BRUTUS
No, Cassius; for the eye sees not itself,
But by reflection, by some other things.
CASSIUS
'Tis just:
And it is very much lamented, Brutus,
That you have no such mirrors as will turn
Your hidden worthiness into your eye,
That you might see your shadow. I have heard,
Where many of the best respect in Rome,
Except immortal Caesar, speaking of Brutus
And groaning underneath this age's yoke,
Have wish'd that noble Brutus had his eyes.
BRUTUS
Into what dangers would you lead me, Cassius,
That you would have me seek into myself
For that which is not in me?
CASSIUS
Therefore, good Brutus, be prepared to hear:
And since you know you cannot see yourself
So well as by reflection, I, your glass,
Will modestly discover to yourself
That of yourself which you yet know not of.
And be not jealous on me, gentle Brutus:
Were I a common laugher, or did use
To stale with ordinary oaths my love
To every new protester; if you know
That I do fawn on men and hug them hard
And after scandal them, or if you know
That I profess myself in banqueting
To all the rout, then hold me dangerous.

Flourish, and shout

BRUTUS

What means this shouting? I do fear, the people
Choose Caesar for their king.
CASSIUS
    Ay, do you fear it?
Then must I think you would not have it so.
BRUTUS
    I would not, Cassius; yet I love him well.
But wherefore do you hold me here so long?
What is it that you would impart to me?
If it be aught toward the general good,
Set honour in one eye and death i' the other,
And I will look on both indifferently,
For let the gods so speed me as I love
The name of honour more than I fear death.
CASSIUS
    I know that virtue to be in you, Brutus,
As well as I do know your outward favour.
Well, honour is the subject of my story.
I cannot tell what you and other men
Think of this life; but, for my single self,
I had as lief not be as live to be
In awe of such a thing as I myself.
I was born free as Caesar; so were you:
We both have fed as well, and we can both
Endure the winter's cold as well as he:
For once, upon a raw and gusty day,
The troubled Tiber chafing with her shores,
Caesar said to me 'Darest thou, Cassius, now
Leap in with me into this angry flood,
And swim to yonder point?' Upon the word,
Accoutred as I was, I plunged in
And bade him follow; so indeed he did.
The torrent roar'd, and we did buffet it
With lusty sinews, throwing it aside

14

And stemming it with hearts of controversy;
But ere we could arrive the point proposed,
Caesar cried 'Help me, Cassius, or I sink!'
I, as Aeneas, our great ancestor,
Did from the flames of Troy upon his shoulder
The old Anchises bear, so from the waves of Tiber
Did I the tired Caesar. And this man
Is now become a god, and Cassius is
A wretched creature and must bend his body,
If Caesar carelessly but nod on him.
He had a fever when he was in Spain,
And when the fit was on him, I did mark
How he did shake: 'tis true, this god did shake;
His coward lips did from their colour fly,
And that same eye whose bend doth awe the world
Did lose his lustre: I did hear him groan:
Ay, and that tongue of his that bade the Romans
Mark him and write his speeches in their books,
Alas, it cried 'Give me some drink, Titinius,'
As a sick girl. Ye gods, it doth amaze me
A man of such a feeble temper should
So get the start of the majestic world
And bear the palm alone.

Shout. Flourish

BRUTUS
Another general shout!
I do believe that these applauses are
For some new honours that are heap'd on Caesar.
CASSIUS
Why, man, he doth bestride the narrow world
Like a Colossus, and we petty men
Walk under his huge legs and peep about
To find ourselves dishonourable graves.

Men at some time are masters of their fates:
The fault, dear Brutus, is not in our stars,
But in ourselves, that we are underlings.
Brutus and Caesar: what should be in that 'Caesar'?
Why should that name be sounded more than yours?
Write them together, yours is as fair a name;
Sound them, it doth become the mouth as well;
Weigh them, it is as heavy; conjure with 'em,
Brutus will start a spirit as soon as Caesar.
Now, in the names of all the gods at once,
Upon what meat doth this our Caesar feed,
That he is grown so great? Age, thou art shamed!
Rome, thou hast lost the breed of noble bloods!
When went there by an age, since the great flood,
But it was famed with more than with one man?
When could they say till now, that talk'd of Rome,
That her wide walls encompass'd but one man?
Now is it Rome indeed and room enough,
When there is in it but one only man.
O, you and I have heard our fathers say,
There was a Brutus once that would have brook'd
The eternal devil to keep his state in Rome
As easily as a king.

BRUTUS

That you do love me, I am nothing jealous;
What you would work me to, I have some aim:
How I have thought of this and of these times,
I shall recount hereafter; for this present,
I would not, so with love I might entreat you,
Be any further moved. What you have said
I will consider; what you have to say
I will with patience hear, and find a time
Both meet to hear and answer such high things.
Till then, my noble friend, chew upon this:

Brutus had rather be a villager
Than to repute himself a son of Rome
Under these hard conditions as this time
Is like to lay upon us.
CASSIUS
I am glad that my weak words
Have struck but thus much show of fire from Brutus.
BRUTUS
The games are done and Caesar is returning.
CASSIUS
As they pass by, pluck Casca by the sleeve;
And he will, after his sour fashion, tell you
What hath proceeded worthy note to-day.

Re-enter CAESAR and his Train

BRUTUS
I will do so. But, look you, Cassius,
The angry spot doth glow on Caesar's brow,
And all the rest look like a chidden train:
Calpurnia's cheek is pale; and Cicero
Looks with such ferret and such fiery eyes
As we have seen him in the Capitol,
Being cross'd in conference by some senators.
CASSIUS
Casca will tell us what the matter is.
CAESAR
Antonius!
ANTONY
Caesar?
CAESAR
Let me have men about me that are fat;
Sleek-headed men and such as sleep o' nights:
Yond Cassius has a lean and hungry look;
He thinks too much: such men are dangerous.

ANTONY
> Fear him not, Caesar; he's not dangerous;
> He is a noble Roman and well given.

CAESAR
> Would he were fatter! But I fear him not:
> Yet if my name were liable to fear,
> I do not know the man I should avoid
> So soon as that spare Cassius. He reads much;
> He is a great observer and he looks
> Quite through the deeds of men: he loves no plays,
> As thou dost, Antony; he hears no music;
> Seldom he smiles, and smiles in such a sort
> As if he mock'd himself and scorn'd his spirit
> That could be moved to smile at any thing.
> Such men as he be never at heart's ease
> Whiles they behold a greater than themselves,
> And therefore are they very dangerous.
> I rather tell thee what is to be fear'd
> Than what I fear; for always I am Caesar.
> Come on my right hand, for this ear is deaf,
> And tell me truly what thou think'st of him.

> *Sennet. Exeunt CAESAR and all his Train, but CASCA*

CASCA
> You pull'd me by the cloak; would you speak with me?

BRUTUS
> Ay, Casca; tell us what hath chanced to-day,
> That Caesar looks so sad.

CASCA
> Why, you were with him, were you not?

BRUTUS
> I should not then ask Casca what had chanced.

CASCA
> Why, there was a crown offered him: and being

offered him, he put it by with the back of his hand,
thus; and then the people fell a-shouting.

BRUTUS

What was the second noise for?

CASCA

Why, for that too.

CASSIUS

They shouted thrice: what was the last cry for?

CASCA

Why, for that too.

BRUTUS

Was the crown offered him thrice?

CASCA

Ay, marry, was't, and he put it by thrice, every
time gentler than other, and at every putting-by
mine honest neighbours shouted.

CASSIUS

Who offered him the crown?

CASCA

Why, Antony.

BRUTUS

Tell us the manner of it, gentle Casca.

CASCA

I can as well be hanged as tell the manner of it:
it was mere foolery; I did not mark it. I saw Mark
Antony offer him a crown;--yet 'twas not a crown
neither, 'twas one of these coronets;--and, as I told
you, he put it by once: but, for all that, to my
thinking, he would fain have had it. Then he
offered it to him again; then he put it by again:
but, to my thinking, he was very loath to lay his
fingers off it. And then he offered it the third
time; he put it the third time by: and still as he
refused it, the rabblement hooted and clapped their

chapped hands and threw up their sweaty night-caps
and uttered such a deal of stinking breath because
Caesar refused the crown that it had almost choked
Caesar; for he swounded and fell down at it: and
for mine own part, I durst not laugh, for fear of
opening my lips and receiving the bad air.

CASSIUS

But, soft, I pray you: what, did Caesar swound?

CASCA

He fell down in the market-place, and foamed at
mouth, and was speechless.

BRUTUS

'Tis very like: he hath the failing sickness.

CASSIUS

No, Caesar hath it not; but you and I,
And honest Casca, we have the falling sickness.

CASCA

I know not what you mean by that; but, I am sure,
Caesar fell down. If the tag-rag people did not
clap him and hiss him, according as he pleased and
displeased them, as they use to do the players in
the theatre, I am no true man.

BRUTUS

What said he when he came unto himself?

CASCA

Marry, before he fell down, when he perceived the
common herd was glad he refused the crown, he
plucked me ope his doublet and offered them his
throat to cut. An I had been a man of any
occupation, if I would not have taken him at a word,
I would I might go to hell among the rogues. And so
he fell. When he came to himself again, he said,
If he had done or said any thing amiss, he desired
their worships to think it was his infirmity. Three

or four wenches, where I stood, cried 'Alas, good
soul!' and forgave him with all their hearts: but
there's no heed to be taken of them; if Caesar had
stabbed their mothers, they would have done no less.
BRUTUS
And after that, he came, thus sad, away?
CASCA
Ay.
CASSIUS
Did Cicero say any thing?
CASCA
Ay, he spoke Greek.
CASSIUS
To what effect?
CASCA
Nay, an I tell you that, Ill ne'er look you i' the
face again: but those that understood him smiled at
one another and shook their heads; but, for mine own
part, it was Greek to me. I could tell you more
news too: Marullus and Flavius, for pulling scarfs
off Caesar's images, are put to silence. Fare you
well. There was more foolery yet, if I could
remember it.
CASSIUS
Will you sup with me to-night, Casca?
CASCA
No, I am promised forth.
CASSIUS
Will you dine with me to-morrow?
CASCA
Ay, if I be alive and your mind hold and your dinner
worth the eating.
CASSIUS
Good: I will expect you.

CASCA
Do so. Farewell, both.

Exit

BRUTUS
What a blunt fellow is this grown to be!
He was quick mettle when he went to school.
CASSIUS
So is he now in execution
Of any bold or noble enterprise,
However he puts on this tardy form.
This rudeness is a sauce to his good wit,
Which gives men stomach to digest his words
With better appetite.
BRUTUS
And so it is. For this time I will leave you:
To-morrow, if you please to speak with me,
I will come home to you; or, if you will,
Come home to me, and I will wait for you.
CASSIUS
I will do so: till then, think of the world.

Exit BRUTUS

Well, Brutus, thou art noble; yet, I see,
Thy honourable metal may be wrought
From that it is disposed: therefore it is meet
That noble minds keep ever with their likes;
For who so firm that cannot be seduced?
Caesar doth bear me hard; but he loves Brutus:
If I were Brutus now and he were Cassius,
He should not humour me. I will this night,
In several hands, in at his windows throw,
As if they came from several citizens,

22

Writings all tending to the great opinion
That Rome holds of his name; wherein obscurely
Caesar's ambition shall be glanced at:
And after this let Caesar seat him sure;
For we will shake him, or worse days endure.

Exit

SCENE III.

The same. A street.

*Thunder and lightning. Enter from opposite sides, CASCA,
with his sword drawn, and CICERO*

CICERO
  Good even, Casca: brought you Caesar home?
  Why are you breathless? and why stare you so?
CASCA
  Are not you moved, when all the sway of earth
  Shakes like a thing unfirm? O Cicero,
  I have seen tempests, when the scolding winds
  Have rived the knotty oaks, and I have seen
  The ambitious ocean swell and rage and foam,
  To be exalted with the threatening clouds:
  But never till to-night, never till now,
  Did I go through a tempest dropping fire.
  Either there is a civil strife in heaven,
  Or else the world, too saucy with the gods,
  Incenses them to send destruction.
CICERO
  Why, saw you any thing more wonderful?
CASCA
  A common slave--you know him well by sight--
  Held up his left hand, which did flame and burn
  Like twenty torches join'd, and yet his hand,

23

Not sensible of fire, remain'd unscorch'd.
Besides--I ha' not since put up my sword--
Against the Capitol I met a lion,
Who glared upon me, and went surly by,
Without annoying me: and there were drawn
Upon a heap a hundred ghastly women,
Transformed with their fear; who swore they saw
Men all in fire walk up and down the streets.
And yesterday the bird of night did sit
Even at noon-day upon the market-place,
Hooting and shrieking. When these prodigies
Do so conjointly meet, let not men say
'These are their reasons; they are natural;'
For, I believe, they are portentous things
Unto the climate that they point upon.

CICERO
Indeed, it is a strange-disposed time:
But men may construe things after their fashion,
Clean from the purpose of the things themselves.
Come Caesar to the Capitol to-morrow?

CASCA
He doth; for he did bid Antonius
Send word to you he would be there to-morrow.

CICERO
Good night then, Casca: this disturbed sky
Is not to walk in.

CASCA
Farewell, Cicero.

Exit CICERO

Enter CASSIUS

CASSIUS

Who's there?
CASCA
A Roman.
CASSIUS
Casca, by your voice.
CASCA
Your ear is good. Cassius, what night is this!
CASSIUS
A very pleasing night to honest men.
CASCA
Who ever knew the heavens menace so?
CASSIUS
Those that have known the earth so full of faults.
For my part, I have walk'd about the streets,
Submitting me unto the perilous night,
And, thus unbraced, Casca, as you see,
Have bared my bosom to the thunder-stone;
And when the cross blue lightning seem'd to open
The breast of heaven, I did present myself
Even in the aim and very flash of it.
CASCA
But wherefore did you so much tempt the heavens?
It is the part of men to fear and tremble,
When the most mighty gods by tokens send
Such dreadful heralds to astonish us.
CASSIUS
You are dull, Casca, and those sparks of life
That should be in a Roman you do want,
Or else you use not. You look pale and gaze
And put on fear and cast yourself in wonder,
To see the strange impatience of the heavens:
But if you would consider the true cause
Why all these fires, why all these gliding ghosts,
Why birds and beasts from quality and kind,

Why old men fool and children calculate,
Why all these things change from their ordinance
Their natures and preformed faculties
To monstrous quality,--why, you shall find
That heaven hath infused them with these spirits,
To make them instruments of fear and warning
Unto some monstrous state.
Now could I, Casca, name to thee a man
Most like this dreadful night,
That thunders, lightens, opens graves, and roars
As doth the lion in the Capitol,
A man no mightier than thyself or me
In personal action, yet prodigious grown
And fearful, as these strange eruptions are.
CASCA
'Tis Caesar that you mean; is it not, Cassius?
CASSIUS
Let it be who it is: for Romans now
Have thews and limbs like to their ancestors;
But, woe the while! our fathers' minds are dead,
And we are govern'd with our mothers' spirits;
Our yoke and sufferance show us womanish.
CASCA
Indeed, they say the senators tomorrow
Mean to establish Caesar as a king;
And he shall wear his crown by sea and land,
In every place, save here in Italy.
CASSIUS
I know where I will wear this dagger then;
Cassius from bondage will deliver Cassius:
Therein, ye gods, you make the weak most strong;
Therein, ye gods, you tyrants do defeat:
Nor stony tower, nor walls of beaten brass,
Nor airless dungeon, nor strong links of iron,

Can be retentive to the strength of spirit;
But life, being weary of these worldly bars,
Never lacks power to dismiss itself.
If I know this, know all the world besides,
That part of tyranny that I do bear
I can shake off at pleasure.

Thunder still

CASCA
So can I:
So every bondman in his own hand bears
The power to cancel his captivity.
CASSIUS
And why should Caesar be a tyrant then?
Poor man! I know he would not be a wolf,
But that he sees the Romans are but sheep:
He were no lion, were not Romans hinds.
Those that with haste will make a mighty fire
Begin it with weak straws: what trash is Rome,
What rubbish and what offal, when it serves
For the base matter to illuminate
So vile a thing as Caesar! But, O grief,
Where hast thou led me? I perhaps speak this
Before a willing bondman; then I know
My answer must be made. But I am arm'd,
And dangers are to me indifferent.
CASCA
You speak to Casca, and to such a man
That is no fleering tell-tale. Hold, my hand:
Be factious for redress of all these griefs,
And I will set this foot of mine as far
As who goes farthest.
CASSIUS
There's a bargain made.

Now know you, Casca, I have moved already
Some certain of the noblest-minded Romans
To undergo with me an enterprise
Of honourable-dangerous consequence;
And I do know, by this, they stay for me
In Pompey's porch: for now, this fearful night,
There is no stir or walking in the streets;
And the complexion of the element
In favour's like the work we have in hand,
Most bloody, fiery, and most terrible.
CASCA
Stand close awhile, for here comes one in haste.
CASSIUS
'Tis Cinna; I do know him by his gait;
He is a friend.

Enter CINNA

Cinna, where haste you so?
CINNA
To find out you. Who's that? Metellus Cimber?
CASSIUS
No, it is Casca; one incorporate
To our attempts. Am I not stay'd for, Cinna?
CINNA
I am glad on 't. What a fearful night is this!
There's two or three of us have seen strange sights.
CASSIUS
Am I not stay'd for? tell me.
CINNA
Yes, you are.
O Cassius, if you could
But win the noble Brutus to our party--
CASSIUS
Be you content: good Cinna, take this paper,

And look you lay it in the praetor's chair,
Where Brutus may but find it; and throw this
In at his window; set this up with wax
Upon old Brutus' statue: all this done,
Repair to Pompey's porch, where you shall find us.
Is Decius Brutus and Trebonius there?
CINNA
All but Metellus Cimber; and he's gone
To seek you at your house. Well, I will hie,
And so bestow these papers as you bade me.
CASSIUS
That done, repair to Pompey's theatre.

Exit CINNA

Come, Casca, you and I will yet ere day
See Brutus at his house: three parts of him
Is ours already, and the man entire
Upon the next encounter yields him ours.
CASCA
O, he sits high in all the people's hearts:
And that which would appear offence in us,
His countenance, like richest alchemy,
Will change to virtue and to worthiness.
CASSIUS
Him and his worth and our great need of him
You have right well conceited. Let us go,
For it is after midnight; and ere day
We will awake him and be sure of him.

Exeunt

ACT II

SCENE I.

Rome. BRUTUS's orchard.

Enter BRUTUS

BRUTUS
What, Lucius, ho!
I cannot, by the progress of the stars,
Give guess how near to day. Lucius, I say!
I would it were my fault to sleep so soundly.
When, Lucius, when? awake, I say! what, Lucius!

Enter LUCIUS

LUCIUS
Call'd you, my lord?
BRUTUS
Get me a taper in my study, Lucius:
When it is lighted, come and call me here.
LUCIUS
I will, my lord.

Exit

BRUTUS
It must be by his death: and for my part,
I know no personal cause to spurn at him,
But for the general. He would be crown'd:
How that might change his nature, there's the question.
It is the bright day that brings forth the adder;
And that craves wary walking. Crown him?--that;--
And then, I grant, we put a sting in him,
That at his will he may do danger with.

The abuse of greatness is, when it disjoins
Remorse from power: and, to speak truth of Caesar,
I have not known when his affections sway'd
More than his reason. But 'tis a common proof,
That lowliness is young ambition's ladder,
Whereto the climber-upward turns his face;
But when he once attains the upmost round.
He then unto the ladder turns his back,
Looks in the clouds, scorning the base degrees
By which he did ascend. So Caesar may.
Then, lest he may, prevent. And, since the quarrel
Will bear no colour for the thing he is,
Fashion it thus; that what he is, augmented,
Would run to these and these extremities:
And therefore think him as a serpent's egg
Which, hatch'd, would, as his kind, grow mischievous,
And kill him in the shell.

Re-enter LUCIUS

LUCIUS
    The taper burneth in your closet, sir.
    Searching the window for a flint, I found
    This paper, thus seal'd up; and, I am sure,
    It did not lie there when I went to bed.

Gives him the letter

BRUTUS
    Get you to bed again; it is not day.
    Is not to-morrow, boy, the ides of March?
LUCIUS
    I know not, sir.
BRUTUS
    Look in the calendar, and bring me word.

LUCIUS
I will, sir.

Exit

BRUTUS
The exhalations whizzing in the air
Give so much light that I may read by them.

Opens the letter and reads

'Brutus, thou sleep'st: awake, and see thyself.
Shall Rome, & c. Speak, strike, redress!
Brutus, thou sleep'st: awake!'
Such instigations have been often dropp'd
Where I have took them up.
'Shall Rome, & c.' Thus must I piece it out:
Shall Rome stand under one man's awe? What, Rome?
My ancestors did from the streets of Rome
The Tarquin drive, when he was call'd a king.
'Speak, strike, redress!' Am I entreated
To speak and strike? O Rome, I make thee promise:
If the redress will follow, thou receivest
Thy full petition at the hand of Brutus!

Re-enter LUCIUS

LUCIUS
Sir, March is wasted fourteen days.

Knocking within

BRUTUS
'Tis good. Go to the gate; somebody knocks.

Exit LUCIUS

Since Cassius first did whet me against Caesar,
I have not slept.
Between the acting of a dreadful thing
And the first motion, all the interim is
Like a phantasma, or a hideous dream:
The Genius and the mortal instruments
Are then in council; and the state of man,
Like to a little kingdom, suffers then
The nature of an insurrection.

Re-enter LUCIUS

LUCIUS
  Sir, 'tis your brother Cassius at the door,
  Who doth desire to see you.
BRUTUS
  Is he alone?
LUCIUS
  No, sir, there are moe with him.
BRUTUS
  Do you know them?
LUCIUS
  No, sir; their hats are pluck'd about their ears,
  And half their faces buried in their cloaks,
  That by no means I may discover them
  By any mark of favour.
BRUTUS
  Let 'em enter.

Exit LUCIUS

They are the faction. O conspiracy,
Shamest thou to show thy dangerous brow by night,
When evils are most free? O, then by day
Where wilt thou find a cavern dark enough

To mask thy monstrous visage? Seek none, conspiracy;
Hide it in smiles and affability:
For if thou path, thy native semblance on,
Not Erebus itself were dim enough
To hide thee from prevention.

Enter the conspirators, CASSIUS, CASCA, DECIUS
BRUTUS, CINNA, METELLUS CIMBER, and TREBONIUS

CASSIUS
I think we are too bold upon your rest:
Good morrow, Brutus; do we trouble you?
BRUTUS
I have been up this hour, awake all night.
Know I these men that come along with you?
CASSIUS
Yes, every man of them, and no man here
But honours you; and every one doth wish
You had but that opinion of yourself
Which every noble Roman bears of you.
This is Trebonius.
BRUTUS
He is welcome hither.
CASSIUS
This, Decius Brutus.
BRUTUS
He is welcome too.
CASSIUS
This, Casca; this, Cinna; and this, Metellus Cimber.
BRUTUS
They are all welcome.
What watchful cares do interpose themselves
Betwixt your eyes and night?
CASSIUS
Shall I entreat a word?

BRUTUS and CASSIUS whisper

DECIUS BRUTUS
  Here lies the east: doth not the day break here?
CASCA
  No.
CINNA
  O, pardon, sir, it doth; and yon gray lines
  That fret the clouds are messengers of day.
CASCA
  You shall confess that you are both deceived.
  Here, as I point my sword, the sun arises,
  Which is a great way growing on the south,
  Weighing the youthful season of the year.
  Some two months hence up higher toward the north
  He first presents his fire; and the high east
  Stands, as the Capitol, directly here.
BRUTUS
  Give me your hands all over, one by one.
CASSIUS
  And let us swear our resolution.
BRUTUS
  No, not an oath: if not the face of men,
  The sufferance of our souls, the time's abuse,--
  If these be motives weak, break off betimes,
  And every man hence to his idle bed;
  So let high-sighted tyranny range on,
  Till each man drop by lottery. But if these,
  As I am sure they do, bear fire enough
  To kindle cowards and to steel with valour
  The melting spirits of women, then, countrymen,
  What need we any spur but our own cause,
  To prick us to redress? what other bond
  Than secret Romans, that have spoke the word,

And will not palter? and what other oath
Than honesty to honesty engaged,
That this shall be, or we will fall for it?
Swear priests and cowards and men cautelous,
Old feeble carrions and such suffering souls
That welcome wrongs; unto bad causes swear
Such creatures as men doubt; but do not stain
The even virtue of our enterprise,
Nor the insuppressive mettle of our spirits,
To think that or our cause or our performance
Did need an oath; when every drop of blood
That every Roman bears, and nobly bears,
Is guilty of a several bastardy,
If he do break the smallest particle
Of any promise that hath pass'd from him.

CASSIUS
But what of Cicero? shall we sound him?
I think he will stand very strong with us.

CASCA
Let us not leave him out.

CINNA
No, by no means.

METELLUS CIMBER
O, let us have him, for his silver hairs
Will purchase us a good opinion
And buy men's voices to commend our deeds:
It shall be said, his judgment ruled our hands;
Our youths and wildness shall no whit appear,
But all be buried in his gravity.

BRUTUS
O, name him not: let us not break with him;
For he will never follow any thing
That other men begin.

CASSIUS

Then leave him out.
CASCA
  Indeed he is not fit.
DECIUS BRUTUS
  Shall no man else be touch'd but only Caesar?
CASSIUS
  Decius, well urged: I think it is not meet,
  Mark Antony, so well beloved of Caesar,
  Should outlive Caesar: we shall find of him
  A shrewd contriver; and, you know, his means,
  If he improve them, may well stretch so far
  As to annoy us all: which to prevent,
  Let Antony and Caesar fall together.
BRUTUS
  Our course will seem too bloody, Caius Cassius,
  To cut the head off and then hack the limbs,
  Like wrath in death and envy afterwards;
  For Antony is but a limb of Caesar:
  Let us be sacrificers, but not butchers, Caius.
  We all stand up against the spirit of Caesar;
  And in the spirit of men there is no blood:
  O, that we then could come by Caesar's spirit,
  And not dismember Caesar! But, alas,
  Caesar must bleed for it! And, gentle friends,
  Let's kill him boldly, but not wrathfully;
  Let's carve him as a dish fit for the gods,
  Not hew him as a carcass fit for hounds:
  And let our hearts, as subtle masters do,
  Stir up their servants to an act of rage,
  And after seem to chide 'em. This shall make
  Our purpose necessary and not envious:
  Which so appearing to the common eyes,
  We shall be call'd purgers, not murderers.
  And for Mark Antony, think not of him;

For he can do no more than Caesar's arm
When Caesar's head is off.
CASSIUS
Yet I fear him;
For in the ingrafted love he bears to Caesar--
BRUTUS
Alas, good Cassius, do not think of him:
If he love Caesar, all that he can do
Is to himself, take thought and die for Caesar:
And that were much he should; for he is given
To sports, to wildness and much company.
TREBONIUS
There is no fear in him; let him not die;
For he will live, and laugh at this hereafter.

Clock strikes

BRUTUS
Peace! count the clock.
CASSIUS
The clock hath stricken three.
TREBONIUS
'Tis time to part.
CASSIUS
But it is doubtful yet,
Whether Caesar will come forth to-day, or no;
For he is superstitious grown of late,
Quite from the main opinion he held once
Of fantasy, of dreams and ceremonies:
It may be, these apparent prodigies,
The unaccustom'd terror of this night,
And the persuasion of his augurers,
May hold him from the Capitol to-day.
DECIUS BRUTUS
Never fear that: if he be so resolved,

I can o'ersway him; for he loves to hear
That unicorns may be betray'd with trees,
And bears with glasses, elephants with holes,
Lions with toils and men with flatterers;
But when I tell him he hates flatterers,
He says he does, being then most flattered.
Let me work;
For I can give his humour the true bent,
And I will bring him to the Capitol.

CASSIUS
Nay, we will all of us be there to fetch him.

BRUTUS
By the eighth hour: is that the uttermost?

CINNA
Be that the uttermost, and fail not then.

METELLUS CIMBER
Caius Ligarius doth bear Caesar hard,
Who rated him for speaking well of Pompey:
I wonder none of you have thought of him.

BRUTUS
Now, good Metellus, go along by him:
He loves me well, and I have given him reasons;
Send him but hither, and I'll fashion him.

CASSIUS
The morning comes upon 's: we'll leave you, Brutus.
And, friends, disperse yourselves; but all remember
What you have said, and show yourselves true Romans.

BRUTUS
Good gentlemen, look fresh and merrily;
Let not our looks put on our purposes,
But bear it as our Roman actors do,
With untired spirits and formal constancy:
And so good morrow to you every one.

Exeunt all but BRUTUS

39

Boy! Lucius! Fast asleep? It is no matter;
Enjoy the honey-heavy dew of slumber:
Thou hast no figures nor no fantasies,
Which busy care draws in the brains of men;
Therefore thou sleep'st so sound.

Enter PORTIA

PORTIA
Brutus, my lord!
BRUTUS
Portia, what mean you? wherefore rise you now?
It is not for your health thus to commit
Your weak condition to the raw cold morning.
PORTIA
Nor for yours neither. You've ungently, Brutus,
Stole from my bed: and yesternight, at supper,
You suddenly arose, and walk'd about,
Musing and sighing, with your arms across,
And when I ask'd you what the matter was,
You stared upon me with ungentle looks;
I urged you further; then you scratch'd your head,
And too impatiently stamp'd with your foot;
Yet I insisted, yet you answer'd not,
But, with an angry wafture of your hand,
Gave sign for me to leave you: so I did;
Fearing to strengthen that impatience
Which seem'd too much enkindled, and withal
Hoping it was but an effect of humour,
Which sometime hath his hour with every man.
It will not let you eat, nor talk, nor sleep,
And could it work so much upon your shape
As it hath much prevail'd on your condition,
I should not know you, Brutus. Dear my lord,

Make me acquainted with your cause of grief.
BRUTUS
    I am not well in health, and that is all.
PORTIA
    Brutus is wise, and, were he not in health,
    He would embrace the means to come by it.
BRUTUS
    Why, so I do. Good Portia, go to bed.
PORTIA
    Is Brutus sick? and is it physical
    To walk unbraced and suck up the humours
    Of the dank morning? What, is Brutus sick,
    And will he steal out of his wholesome bed,
    To dare the vile contagion of the night
    And tempt the rheumy and unpurged air
    To add unto his sickness? No, my Brutus;
    You have some sick offence within your mind,
    Which, by the right and virtue of my place,
    I ought to know of: and, upon my knees,
    I charm you, by my once-commended beauty,
    By all your vows of love and that great vow
    Which did incorporate and make us one,
    That you unfold to me, yourself, your half,
    Why you are heavy, and what men to-night
    Have had to resort to you: for here have been
    Some six or seven, who did hide their faces
    Even from darkness.
BRUTUS
    Kneel not, gentle Portia.
PORTIA
    I should not need, if you were gentle Brutus.
    Within the bond of marriage, tell me, Brutus,
    Is it excepted I should know no secrets
    That appertain to you? Am I yourself

But, as it were, in sort or limitation,
To keep with you at meals, comfort your bed,
And talk to you sometimes? Dwell I but in the suburbs
Of your good pleasure? If it be no more,
Portia is Brutus' harlot, not his wife.

BRUTUS

You are my true and honourable wife,
As dear to me as are the ruddy drops
That visit my sad heart

PORTIA

If this were true, then should I know this secret.
I grant I am a woman; but withal
A woman that Lord Brutus took to wife:
I grant I am a woman; but withal
A woman well-reputed, Cato's daughter.
Think you I am no stronger than my sex,
Being so father'd and so husbanded?
Tell me your counsels, I will not disclose 'em:
I have made strong proof of my constancy,
Giving myself a voluntary wound
Here, in the thigh: can I bear that with patience.
And not my husband's secrets?

BRUTUS

O ye gods,
Render me worthy of this noble wife!

Knocking within

Hark, hark! one knocks: Portia, go in awhile;
And by and by thy bosom shall partake
The secrets of my heart.
All my engagements I will construe to thee,
All the charactery of my sad brows:
Leave me with haste.

42

Exit PORTIA

Lucius, who's that knocks?

Re-enter LUCIUS with LIGARIUS

LUCIUS
He is a sick man that would speak with you.
BRUTUS
Caius Ligarius, that Metellus spake of.
Boy, stand aside. Caius Ligarius! how?
LIGARIUS
Vouchsafe good morrow from a feeble tongue.
BRUTUS
O, what a time have you chose out, brave Caius,
To wear a kerchief! Would you were not sick!
LIGARIUS
I am not sick, if Brutus have in hand
Any exploit worthy the name of honour.
BRUTUS
Such an exploit have I in hand, Ligarius,
Had you a healthful ear to hear of it.
LIGARIUS
By all the gods that Romans bow before,
I here discard my sickness! Soul of Rome!
Brave son, derived from honourable loins!
Thou, like an exorcist, hast conjured up
My mortified spirit. Now bid me run,
And I will strive with things impossible;
Yea, get the better of them. What's to do?
BRUTUS
A piece of work that will make sick men whole.
LIGARIUS
But are not some whole that we must make sick?
BRUTUS

43

That must we also. What it is, my Caius,
I shall unfold to thee, as we are going
To whom it must be done.
LIGARIUS
Set on your foot,
And with a heart new-fired I follow you,
To do I know not what: but it sufficeth
That Brutus leads me on.
BRUTUS
Follow me, then.

Exeunt

SCENE II.

CAESAR's house.

Thunder and lightning. Enter CAESAR, in his night-gown

CAESAR
Nor heaven nor earth have been at peace to-night:
Thrice hath Calpurnia in her sleep cried out,
'Help, ho! they murder Caesar!' Who's within?

Enter a Servant

Servant
My lord?
CAESAR
Go bid the priests do present sacrifice
And bring me their opinions of success.
Servant
I will, my lord.

Exit

Enter CALPURNIA

CALPURNIA
    What mean you, Caesar? think you to walk forth?
    You shall not stir out of your house to-day.
CAESAR
    Caesar shall forth: the things that threaten'd me
    Ne'er look'd but on my back; when they shall see
    The face of Caesar, they are vanished.
CALPURNIA
    Caesar, I never stood on ceremonies,
    Yet now they fright me. There is one within,
    Besides the things that we have heard and seen,
    Recounts most horrid sights seen by the watch.
    A lioness hath whelped in the streets;
    And graves have yawn'd, and yielded up their dead;
    Fierce fiery warriors fought upon the clouds,
    In ranks and squadrons and right form of war,
    Which drizzled blood upon the Capitol;
    The noise of battle hurtled in the air,
    Horses did neigh, and dying men did groan,
    And ghosts did shriek and squeal about the streets.
    O Caesar! these things are beyond all use,
    And I do fear them.
CAESAR
    What can be avoided
    Whose end is purposed by the mighty gods?
    Yet Caesar shall go forth; for these predictions
    Are to the world in general as to Caesar.
CALPURNIA
    When beggars die, there are no comets seen;
    The heavens themselves blaze forth the death of princes.
CAESAR
    Cowards die many times before their deaths;
    The valiant never taste of death but once.

Of all the wonders that I yet have heard.
It seems to me most strange that men should fear;
Seeing that death, a necessary end,
Will come when it will come.

Re-enter Servant

What say the augurers?
Servant
They would not have you to stir forth to-day.
Plucking the entrails of an offering forth,
They could not find a heart within the beast.
CAESAR
The gods do this in shame of cowardice:
Caesar should be a beast without a heart,
If he should stay at home to-day for fear.
No, Caesar shall not: danger knows full well
That Caesar is more dangerous than he:
We are two lions litter'd in one day,
And I the elder and more terrible:
And Caesar shall go forth.
CALPURNIA
Alas, my lord,
Your wisdom is consumed in confidence.
Do not go forth to-day: call it my fear
That keeps you in the house, and not your own.
We'll send Mark Antony to the senate-house:
And he shall say you are not well to-day:
Let me, upon my knee, prevail in this.
CAESAR
Mark Antony shall say I am not well,
And, for thy humour, I will stay at home.

Enter DECIUS BRUTUS

Here's Decius Brutus, he shall tell them so.
DECIUS BRUTUS
Caesar, all hail! good morrow, worthy Caesar:
I come to fetch you to the senate-house.
CAESAR
And you are come in very happy time,
To bear my greeting to the senators
And tell them that I will not come to-day:
Cannot, is false, and that I dare not, falser:
I will not come to-day: tell them so, Decius.
CALPURNIA
Say he is sick.
CAESAR
Shall Caesar send a lie?
Have I in conquest stretch'd mine arm so far,
To be afraid to tell graybeards the truth?
Decius, go tell them Caesar will not come.
DECIUS BRUTUS
Most mighty Caesar, let me know some cause,
Lest I be laugh'd at when I tell them so.
CAESAR
The cause is in my will: I will not come;
That is enough to satisfy the senate.
But for your private satisfaction,
Because I love you, I will let you know:
Calpurnia here, my wife, stays me at home:
She dreamt to-night she saw my statua,
Which, like a fountain with an hundred spouts,
Did run pure blood: and many lusty Romans
Came smiling, and did bathe their hands in it:
And these does she apply for warnings, and portents,
And evils imminent; and on her knee
Hath begg'd that I will stay at home to-day.
DECIUS BRUTUS

47

This dream is all amiss interpreted;
It was a vision fair and fortunate:
Your statue spouting blood in many pipes,
In which so many smiling Romans bathed,
Signifies that from you great Rome shall suck
Reviving blood, and that great men shall press
For tinctures, stains, relics and cognizance.
This by Calpurnia's dream is signified.

CAESAR
And this way have you well expounded it.

DECIUS BRUTUS
I have, when you have heard what I can say:
And know it now: the senate have concluded
To give this day a crown to mighty Caesar.
If you shall send them word you will not come,
Their minds may change. Besides, it were a mock
Apt to be render'd, for some one to say
'Break up the senate till another time,
When Caesar's wife shall meet with better dreams.'
If Caesar hide himself, shall they not whisper
'Lo, Caesar is afraid'?
Pardon me, Caesar; for my dear dear love
To our proceeding bids me tell you this;
And reason to my love is liable.

CAESAR
How foolish do your fears seem now, Calpurnia!
I am ashamed I did yield to them.
Give me my robe, for I will go.

Enter PUBLIUS, BRUTUS, LIGARIUS, METELLUS,
CASCA, TREBONIUS, and CINNA

And look where Publius is come to fetch me.

PUBLIUS
Good morrow, Caesar.

CAESAR
  Welcome, Publius.
  What, Brutus, are you stirr'd so early too?
  Good morrow, Casca. Caius Ligarius,
  Caesar was ne'er so much your enemy
  As that same ague which hath made you lean.
  What is 't o'clock?
BRUTUS
  Caesar, 'tis strucken eight.
CAESAR
  I thank you for your pains and courtesy.

Enter ANTONY

  See! Antony, that revels long o' nights,
  Is notwithstanding up. Good morrow, Antony.
ANTONY
  So to most noble Caesar.
CAESAR
  Bid them prepare within:
  I am to blame to be thus waited for.
  Now, Cinna: now, Metellus: what, Trebonius!
  I have an hour's talk in store for you;
  Remember that you call on me to-day:
  Be near me, that I may remember you.
TREBONIUS
  Caesar, I will:

Aside

  and so near will I be,
  That your best friends shall wish I had been further.
CAESAR
  Good friends, go in, and taste some wine with me;
  And we, like friends, will straightway go together.

BRUTUS
[Aside] That every like is not the same, O Caesar,
The heart of Brutus yearns to think upon!

Exeunt

SCENE III.

A street near the Capitol.

Enter ARTEMIDORUS, reading a paper

ARTEMIDORUS
'Caesar, beware of Brutus; take heed of Cassius;
come not near Casca; have an eye to Cinna, trust not
Trebonius: mark well Metellus Cimber: Decius Brutus
loves thee not: thou hast wronged Caius Ligarius.
There is but one mind in all these men, and it is
bent against Caesar. If thou beest not immortal,
look about you: security gives way to conspiracy.
The mighty gods defend thee!
Thy lover,
        'ARTEMIDORUS."

Here will I stand till Caesar pass along,
And as a suitor will I give him this.
My heart laments that virtue cannot live
Out of the teeth of emulation.
If thou read this, O Caesar, thou mayst live;
If not, the Fates with traitors do contrive.

Exit

SCENE IV.

*Another part of the same street, before the house of
BRUTUS.*

Enter PORTIA and LUCIUS

PORTIA
    I prithee, boy, run to the senate-house;
    Stay not to answer me, but get thee gone:
    Why dost thou stay?
LUCIUS
    To know my errand, madam.
PORTIA
    I would have had thee there, and here again,
    Ere I can tell thee what thou shouldst do there.
    O constancy, be strong upon my side,
    Set a huge mountain 'tween my heart and tongue!
    I have a man's mind, but a woman's might.
    How hard it is for women to keep counsel!
    Art thou here yet?
LUCIUS
    Madam, what should I do?
    Run to the Capitol, and nothing else?
    And so return to you, and nothing else?
PORTIA
    Yes, bring me word, boy, if thy lord look well,
    For he went sickly forth: and take good note
    What Caesar doth, what suitors press to him.
    Hark, boy! what noise is that?
LUCIUS
    I hear none, madam.
PORTIA
    Prithee, listen well;
    I heard a bustling rumour, like a fray,
    And the wind brings it from the Capitol.

LUCIUS
Sooth, madam, I hear nothing.

Enter the Soothsayer

PORTIA
Come hither, fellow: which way hast thou been?
Soothsayer
At mine own house, good lady.
PORTIA
What is't o'clock?
Soothsayer
About the ninth hour, lady.
PORTIA
Is Caesar yet gone to the Capitol?
Soothsayer
Madam, not yet: I go to take my stand,
To see him pass on to the Capitol.
PORTIA
Thou hast some suit to Caesar, hast thou not?
Soothsayer
That I have, lady: if it will please Caesar
To be so good to Caesar as to hear me,
I shall beseech him to befriend himself.
PORTIA
Why, know'st thou any harm's intended towards him?
Soothsayer
None that I know will be, much that I fear may chance.
Good morrow to you. Here the street is narrow:
The throng that follows Caesar at the heels,
Of senators, of praetors, common suitors,
Will crowd a feeble man almost to death:
I'll get me to a place more void, and there
Speak to great Caesar as he comes along.

Exit

PORTIA
    I must go in. Ay me, how weak a thing
    The heart of woman is! O Brutus,
    The heavens speed thee in thine enterprise!
    Sure, the boy heard me: Brutus hath a suit
    That Caesar will not grant. O, I grow faint.
    Run, Lucius, and commend me to my lord;
    Say I am merry: come to me again,
    And bring me word what he doth say to thee.

Exeunt severally

ACT III

SCENE I.

Rome. Before the Capitol; the Senate sitting above.

A crowd of people; among them ARTEMIDORUS and the Soothsayer. Flourish. Enter CAESAR, BRUTUS, CASSIUS, CASCA, DECIUS BRUTUS, METELLUS CIMBER, TREBONIUS, CINNA, ANTONY, LEPIDUS, POPILIUS, PUBLIUS, and others

CAESAR
[To the Soothsayer] The ides of March are come.
Soothsayer
Ay, Caesar; but not gone.
ARTEMIDORUS
Hail, Caesar! read this schedule.
DECIUS BRUTUS
Trebonius doth desire you to o'erread,
At your best leisure, this his humble suit.
ARTEMIDORUS
O Caesar, read mine first; for mine's a suit
That touches Caesar nearer: read it, great Caesar.
CAESAR
What touches us ourself shall be last served.
ARTEMIDORUS
Delay not, Caesar; read it instantly.
CAESAR
What, is the fellow mad?
PUBLIUS
Sirrah, give place.
CASSIUS
What, urge you your petitions in the street?
Come to the Capitol.

54

CAESAR goes up to the Senate-House, the rest following

POPILIUS
I wish your enterprise to-day may thrive.
CASSIUS
What enterprise, Popilius?
POPILIUS
Fare you well.

Advances to CAESAR

BRUTUS
What said Popilius Lena?
CASSIUS
He wish'd to-day our enterprise might thrive.
I fear our purpose is discovered.
BRUTUS
Look, how he makes to Caesar; mark him.
CASSIUS
Casca, be sudden, for we fear prevention.
Brutus, what shall be done? If this be known,
Cassius or Caesar never shall turn back,
For I will slay myself.
BRUTUS
Cassius, be constant:
Popilius Lena speaks not of our purposes;
For, look, he smiles, and Caesar doth not change.
CASSIUS
Trebonius knows his time; for, look you, Brutus.
He draws Mark Antony out of the way.

Exeunt ANTONY and TREBONIUS

DECIUS BRUTUS
Where is Metellus Cimber? Let him go,

And presently prefer his suit to Caesar.
BRUTUS
He is address'd: press near and second him.
CINNA
Casca, you are the first that rears your hand.
CAESAR
Are we all ready? What is now amiss
That Caesar and his senate must redress?
METELLUS CIMBER
Most high, most mighty, and most puissant Caesar,
Metellus Cimber throws before thy seat
An humble heart,--

Kneeling

CAESAR
I must prevent thee, Cimber.
These couchings and these lowly courtesies
Might fire the blood of ordinary men,
And turn pre-ordinance and first decree
Into the law of children. Be not fond,
To think that Caesar bears such rebel blood
That will be thaw'd from the true quality
With that which melteth fools; I mean, sweet words,
Low-crooked court'sies and base spaniel-fawning.
Thy brother by decree is banished:
If thou dost bend and pray and fawn for him,
I spurn thee like a cur out of my way.
Know, Caesar doth not wrong, nor without cause
Will he be satisfied.
METELLUS CIMBER
Is there no voice more worthy than my own
To sound more sweetly in great Caesar's ear
For the repealing of my banish'd brother?
BRUTUS

I kiss thy hand, but not in flattery, Caesar;
Desiring thee that Publius Cimber may
Have an immediate freedom of repeal.
CAESAR
What, Brutus!
CASSIUS
Pardon, Caesar; Caesar, pardon:
As low as to thy foot doth Cassius fall,
To beg enfranchisement for Publius Cimber.
CASSIUS
I could be well moved, if I were as you:
If I could pray to move, prayers would move me:
But I am constant as the northern star,
Of whose true-fix'd and resting quality
There is no fellow in the firmament.
The skies are painted with unnumber'd sparks,
They are all fire and every one doth shine,
But there's but one in all doth hold his place:
So in the world; 'tis furnish'd well with men,
And men are flesh and blood, and apprehensive;
Yet in the number I do know but one
That unassailable holds on his rank,
Unshaked of motion: and that I am he,
Let me a little show it, even in this;
That I was constant Cimber should be banish'd,
And constant do remain to keep him so.
CINNA
O Caesar,--
CAESAR
Hence! wilt thou lift up Olympus?
DECIUS BRUTUS
Great Caesar,--
CAESAR
Doth not Brutus bootless kneel?

CASCA
Speak, hands for me!

*CASCA first, then the other Conspirators and BRUTUS stab
CAESAR*

CAESAR
Et tu, Brute! Then fall, Caesar.

Dies

CINNA
Liberty! Freedom! Tyranny is dead!
Run hence, proclaim, cry it about the streets.
CASSIUS
Some to the common pulpits, and cry out
'Liberty, freedom, and enfranchisement!'
BRUTUS
People and senators, be not affrighted;
Fly not; stand stiff: ambition's debt is paid.
CASCA
Go to the pulpit, Brutus.
DECIUS BRUTUS
And Cassius too.
BRUTUS
Where's Publius?
CINNA
Here, quite confounded with this mutiny.
METELLUS CIMBER
Stand fast together, lest some friend of Caesar's
Should chance--
BRUTUS
Talk not of standing. Publius, good cheer;
There is no harm intended to your person,
Nor to no Roman else: so tell them, Publius.

CASSIUS
And leave us, Publius; lest that the people,
Rushing on us, should do your age some mischief.
BRUTUS
Do so: and let no man abide this deed,
But we the doers.

Re-enter TREBONIUS

CASSIUS
Where is Antony?
TREBONIUS
Fled to his house amazed:
Men, wives and children stare, cry out and run
As it were doomsday.
BRUTUS
Fates, we will know your pleasures:
That we shall die, we know; 'tis but the time
And drawing days out, that men stand upon.
CASSIUS
Why, he that cuts off twenty years of life
Cuts off so many years of fearing death.
BRUTUS
Grant that, and then is death a benefit:
So are we Caesar's friends, that have abridged
His time of fearing death. Stoop, Romans, stoop,
And let us bathe our hands in Caesar's blood
Up to the elbows, and besmear our swords:
Then walk we forth, even to the market-place,
And, waving our red weapons o'er our heads,
Let's all cry 'Peace, freedom and liberty!'
CASSIUS
Stoop, then, and wash. How many ages hence
Shall this our lofty scene be acted over
In states unborn and accents yet unknown!

BRUTUS
How many times shall Caesar bleed in sport,
That now on Pompey's basis lies along
No worthier than the dust!
CASSIUS
So oft as that shall be,
So often shall the knot of us be call'd
The men that gave their country liberty.
DECIUS BRUTUS
What, shall we forth?
CASSIUS
Ay, every man away:
Brutus shall lead; and we will grace his heels
With the most boldest and best hearts of Rome.

Enter a Servant

BRUTUS
Soft! who comes here? A friend of Antony's.
Servant
Thus, Brutus, did my master bid me kneel:
Thus did Mark Antony bid me fall down;
And, being prostrate, thus he bade me say:
Brutus is noble, wise, valiant, and honest;
Caesar was mighty, bold, royal, and loving:
Say I love Brutus, and I honour him;
Say I fear'd Caesar, honour'd him and loved him.
If Brutus will vouchsafe that Antony
May safely come to him, and be resolved
How Caesar hath deserved to lie in death,
Mark Antony shall not love Caesar dead
So well as Brutus living; but will follow
The fortunes and affairs of noble Brutus
Thorough the hazards of this untrod state
With all true faith. So says my master Antony.

BRUTUS

    Thy master is a wise and valiant Roman;
    I never thought him worse.
    Tell him, so please him come unto this place,
    He shall be satisfied; and, by my honour,
    Depart untouch'd.

Servant

    I'll fetch him presently.

Exit

BRUTUS

    I know that we shall have him well to friend.

CASSIUS

    I wish we may: but yet have I a mind
    That fears him much; and my misgiving still
    Falls shrewdly to the purpose.

BRUTUS

    But here comes Antony.

Re-enter ANTONY

    Welcome, Mark Antony.

ANTONY

    O mighty Caesar! dost thou lie so low?
    Are all thy conquests, glories, triumphs, spoils,
    Shrunk to this little measure? Fare thee well.
    I know not, gentlemen, what you intend,
    Who else must be let blood, who else is rank:
    If I myself, there is no hour so fit
    As Caesar's death hour, nor no instrument
    Of half that worth as those your swords, made rich
    With the most noble blood of all this world.
    I do beseech ye, if you bear me hard,
    Now, whilst your purpled hands do reek and smoke,

Fulfil your pleasure. Live a thousand years,
I shall not find myself so apt to die:
No place will please me so, no mean of death,
As here by Caesar, and by you cut off,
The choice and master spirits of this age.

BRUTUS

O Antony, beg not your death of us.
Though now we must appear bloody and cruel,
As, by our hands and this our present act,
You see we do, yet see you but our hands
And this the bleeding business they have done:
Our hearts you see not; they are pitiful;
And pity to the general wrong of Rome--
As fire drives out fire, so pity pity--
Hath done this deed on Caesar. For your part,
To you our swords have leaden points, Mark Antony:
Our arms, in strength of malice, and our hearts
Of brothers' temper, do receive you in
With all kind love, good thoughts, and reverence.

CASSIUS

Your voice shall be as strong as any man's
In the disposing of new dignities.

BRUTUS

Only be patient till we have appeased
The multitude, beside themselves with fear,
And then we will deliver you the cause,
Why I, that did love Caesar when I struck him,
Have thus proceeded.

ANTONY

I doubt not of your wisdom.
Let each man render me his bloody hand:
First, Marcus Brutus, will I shake with you;
Next, Caius Cassius, do I take your hand;
Now, Decius Brutus, yours: now yours, Metellus;

Yours, Cinna; and, my valiant Casca, yours;
Though last, not last in love, yours, good Trebonius.
Gentlemen all,--alas, what shall I say?
My credit now stands on such slippery ground,
That one of two bad ways you must conceit me,
Either a coward or a flatterer.
That I did love thee, Caesar, O, 'tis true:
If then thy spirit look upon us now,
Shall it not grieve thee dearer than thy death,
To see thy thy Anthony making his peace,
Shaking the bloody fingers of thy foes,
Most noble! in the presence of thy corse?
Had I as many eyes as thou hast wounds,
Weeping as fast as they stream forth thy blood,
It would become me better than to close
In terms of friendship with thine enemies.
Pardon me, Julius! Here wast thou bay'd, brave hart;
Here didst thou fall; and here thy hunters stand,
Sign'd in thy spoil, and crimson'd in thy lethe.
O world, thou wast the forest to this hart;
And this, indeed, O world, the heart of thee.
How like a deer, strucken by many princes,
Dost thou here lie!
CASSIUS
Mark Antony,--
ANTONY
Pardon me, Caius Cassius:
The enemies of Caesar shall say this;
Then, in a friend, it is cold modesty.
CASSIUS
I blame you not for praising Caesar so;
But what compact mean you to have with us?
Will you be prick'd in number of our friends;
Or shall we on, and not depend on you?

ANTONY
> Therefore I took your hands, but was, indeed,
> Sway'd from the point, by looking down on Caesar.
> Friends am I with you all and love you all,
> Upon this hope, that you shall give me reasons
> Why and wherein Caesar was dangerous.

BRUTUS
> Or else were this a savage spectacle:
> Our reasons are so full of good regard
> That were you, Antony, the son of Caesar,
> You should be satisfied.

ANTONY
> That's all I seek:
> And am moreover suitor that I may
> Produce his body to the market-place;
> And in the pulpit, as becomes a friend,
> Speak in the order of his funeral.

BRUTUS
> You shall, Mark Antony.

CASSIUS
> Brutus, a word with you.

Aside to BRUTUS

> You know not what you do: do not consent
> That Antony speak in his funeral:
> Know you how much the people may be moved
> By that which he will utter?

BRUTUS
> By your pardon;
> I will myself into the pulpit first,
> And show the reason of our Caesar's death:
> What Antony shall speak, I will protest
> He speaks by leave and by permission,
> And that we are contented Caesar shall

Have all true rites and lawful ceremonies.
It shall advantage more than do us wrong.
CASSIUS
    I know not what may fall; I like it not.
BRUTUS
    Mark Antony, here, take you Caesar's body.
    You shall not in your funeral speech blame us,
    But speak all good you can devise of Caesar,
    And say you do't by our permission;
    Else shall you not have any hand at all
    About his funeral: and you shall speak
    In the same pulpit whereto I am going,
    After my speech is ended.
ANTONY
    Be it so.
    I do desire no more.
BRUTUS
    Prepare the body then, and follow us.

Exeunt all but ANTONY

ANTONY
    O, pardon me, thou bleeding piece of earth,
    That I am meek and gentle with these butchers!
    Thou art the ruins of the noblest man
    That ever lived in the tide of times.
    Woe to the hand that shed this costly blood!
    Over thy wounds now do I prophesy,--
    Which, like dumb mouths, do ope their ruby lips,
    To beg the voice and utterance of my tongue--
    A curse shall light upon the limbs of men;
    Domestic fury and fierce civil strife
    Shall cumber all the parts of Italy;
    Blood and destruction shall be so in use
    And dreadful objects so familiar

That mothers shall but smile when they behold
Their infants quarter'd with the hands of war;
All pity choked with custom of fell deeds:
And Caesar's spirit, ranging for revenge,
With Ate by his side come hot from hell,
Shall in these confines with a monarch's voice
Cry 'Havoc,' and let slip the dogs of war;
That this foul deed shall smell above the earth
With carrion men, groaning for burial.

Enter a Servant

You serve Octavius Caesar, do you not?
Servant
I do, Mark Antony.
ANTONY
Caesar did write for him to come to Rome.
Servant
He did receive his letters, and is coming;
And bid me say to you by word of mouth--
O Caesar!--

Seeing the body

ANTONY
Thy heart is big, get thee apart and weep.
Passion, I see, is catching; for mine eyes,
Seeing those beads of sorrow stand in thine,
Began to water. Is thy master coming?
Servant
He lies to-night within seven leagues of Rome.
ANTONY
Post back with speed, and tell him what hath chanced:
Here is a mourning Rome, a dangerous Rome,
No Rome of safety for Octavius yet;

Hie hence, and tell him so. Yet, stay awhile;
Thou shalt not back till I have borne this corse
Into the market-place: there shall I try
In my oration, how the people take
The cruel issue of these bloody men;
According to the which, thou shalt discourse
To young Octavius of the state of things.
Lend me your hand.

Exeunt with CAESAR's body

SCENE II.

The Forum.

Enter BRUTUS and CASSIUS, and a throng of Citizens

Citizens
  We will be satisfied; let us be satisfied.
BRUTUS
  Then follow me, and give me audience, friends.
  Cassius, go you into the other street,
  And part the numbers.
  Those that will hear me speak, let 'em stay here;
  Those that will follow Cassius, go with him;
  And public reasons shall be rendered
  Of Caesar's death.
First Citizen
  I will hear Brutus speak.
Second Citizen
  I will hear Cassius; and compare their reasons,
  When severally we hear them rendered.

*Exit CASSIUS, with some of the Citizens. BRUTUS goes into
the pulpit*

Third Citizen

The noble Brutus is ascended: silence!
BRUTUS
Be patient till the last.
Romans, countrymen, and lovers! hear me for my
cause, and be silent, that you may hear: believe me
for mine honour, and have respect to mine honour, that
you may believe: censure me in your wisdom, and
awake your senses, that you may the better judge.
If there be any in this assembly, any dear friend of
Caesar's, to him I say, that Brutus' love to Caesar
was no less than his. If then that friend demand
why Brutus rose against Caesar, this is my answer:
--Not that I loved Caesar less, but that I loved
Rome more. Had you rather Caesar were living and
die all slaves, than that Caesar were dead, to live
all free men? As Caesar loved me, I weep for him;
as he was fortunate, I rejoice at it; as he was
valiant, I honour him: but, as he was ambitious, I
slew him. There is tears for his love; joy for his
fortune; honour for his valour; and death for his
ambition. Who is here so base that would be a
bondman? If any, speak; for him have I offended.
Who is here so rude that would not be a Roman? If
any, speak; for him have I offended. Who is here so
vile that will not love his country? If any, speak;
for him have I offended. I pause for a reply.
All
None, Brutus, none.
BRUTUS
Then none have I offended. I have done no more to
Caesar than you shall do to Brutus. The question of
his death is enrolled in the Capitol; his glory not
extenuated, wherein he was worthy, nor his offences
enforced, for which he suffered death.

Enter ANTONY and others, with CAESAR's body

Here comes his body, mourned by Mark Antony: who,
though he had no hand in his death, shall receive
the benefit of his dying, a place in the
commonwealth; as which of you shall not? With this
I depart,--that, as I slew my best lover for the
good of Rome, I have the same dagger for myself,
when it shall please my country to need my death.
All
   Live, Brutus! live, live!
First Citizen
   Bring him with triumph home unto his house.
Second Citizen
   Give him a statue with his ancestors.
Third Citizen
   Let him be Caesar.
Fourth Citizen
   Caesar's better parts
   Shall be crown'd in Brutus.
First Citizen
   We'll bring him to his house
   With shouts and clamours.
BRUTUS
   My countrymen,--
Second Citizen
   Peace, silence! Brutus speaks.
First Citizen
   Peace, ho!
BRUTUS
   Good countrymen, let me depart alone,
   And, for my sake, stay here with Antony:
   Do grace to Caesar's corpse, and grace his speech
   Tending to Caesar's glories; which Mark Antony,

By our permission, is allow'd to make.
I do entreat you, not a man depart,
Save I alone, till Antony have spoke.

Exit

First Citizen
Stay, ho! and let us hear Mark Antony.
Third Citizen
Let him go up into the public chair;
We'll hear him. Noble Antony, go up.
ANTONY
For Brutus' sake, I am beholding to you.

Goes into the pulpit

Fourth Citizen
What does he say of Brutus?
Third Citizen
He says, for Brutus' sake,
He finds himself beholding to us all.
Fourth Citizen
'Twere best he speak no harm of Brutus here.
First Citizen
This Caesar was a tyrant.
Third Citizen
Nay, that's certain:
We are blest that Rome is rid of him.
Second Citizen
Peace! let us hear what Antony can say.
ANTONY
You gentle Romans,--
Citizens
Peace, ho! let us hear him.
ANTONY

Friends, Romans, countrymen, lend me your ears;
I come to bury Caesar, not to praise him.
The evil that men do lives after them;
The good is oft interred with their bones;
So let it be with Caesar. The noble Brutus
Hath told you Caesar was ambitious:
If it were so, it was a grievous fault,
And grievously hath Caesar answer'd it.
Here, under leave of Brutus and the rest--
For Brutus is an honourable man;
So are they all, all honourable men--
Come I to speak in Caesar's funeral.
He was my friend, faithful and just to me:
But Brutus says he was ambitious;
And Brutus is an honourable man.
He hath brought many captives home to Rome
Whose ransoms did the general coffers fill:
Did this in Caesar seem ambitious?
When that the poor have cried, Caesar hath wept:
Ambition should be made of sterner stuff:
Yet Brutus says he was ambitious;
And Brutus is an honourable man.
You all did see that on the Lupercal
I thrice presented him a kingly crown,
Which he did thrice refuse: was this ambition?
Yet Brutus says he was ambitious;
And, sure, he is an honourable man.
I speak not to disprove what Brutus spoke,
But here I am to speak what I do know.
You all did love him once, not without cause:
What cause withholds you then, to mourn for him?
O judgment! thou art fled to brutish beasts,
And men have lost their reason. Bear with me;
My heart is in the coffin there with Caesar,

And I must pause till it come back to me.
First Citizen
Methinks there is much reason in his sayings.
Second Citizen
If thou consider rightly of the matter,
Caesar has had great wrong.
Third Citizen
Has he, masters?
I fear there will a worse come in his place.
Fourth Citizen
Mark'd ye his words? He would not take the crown;
Therefore 'tis certain he was not ambitious.
First Citizen
If it be found so, some will dear abide it.
Second Citizen
Poor soul! his eyes are red as fire with weeping.
Third Citizen
There's not a nobler man in Rome than Antony.
Fourth Citizen
Now mark him, he begins again to speak.
ANTONY
But yesterday the word of Caesar might
Have stood against the world; now lies he there.
And none so poor to do him reverence.
O masters, if I were disposed to stir
Your hearts and minds to mutiny and rage,
I should do Brutus wrong, and Cassius wrong,
Who, you all know, are honourable men:
I will not do them wrong; I rather choose
To wrong the dead, to wrong myself and you,
Than I will wrong such honourable men.
But here's a parchment with the seal of Caesar;
I found it in his closet, 'tis his will:
Let but the commons hear this testament--

Which, pardon me, I do not mean to read--
And they would go and kiss dead Caesar's wounds
And dip their napkins in his sacred blood,
Yea, beg a hair of him for memory,
And, dying, mention it within their wills,
Bequeathing it as a rich legacy
Unto their issue.
Fourth Citizen
We'll hear the will: read it, Mark Antony.
All
The will, the will! we will hear Caesar's will.
ANTONY
Have patience, gentle friends, I must not read it;
It is not meet you know how Caesar loved you.
You are not wood, you are not stones, but men;
And, being men, bearing the will of Caesar,
It will inflame you, it will make you mad:
'Tis good you know not that you are his heirs;
For, if you should, O, what would come of it!
Fourth Citizen
Read the will; we'll hear it, Antony;
You shall read us the will, Caesar's will.
ANTONY
Will you be patient? will you stay awhile?
I have o'ershot myself to tell you of it:
I fear I wrong the honourable men
Whose daggers have stabb'd Caesar; I do fear it.
Fourth Citizen
They were traitors: honourable men!
All
The will! the testament!
Second Citizen
They were villains, murderers: the will! read the will.
ANTONY

You will compel me, then, to read the will?
Then make a ring about the corpse of Caesar,
And let me show you him that made the will.
Shall I descend? and will you give me leave?
Several Citizens
  Come down.
Second Citizen
  Descend.
Third Citizen
  You shall have leave.

ANTONY comes down

Fourth Citizen
  A ring; stand round.
First Citizen
  Stand from the hearse, stand from the body.
Second Citizen
  Room for Antony, most noble Antony.
ANTONY
  Nay, press not so upon me; stand far off.
Several Citizens
  Stand back; room; bear back.
ANTONY
  If you have tears, prepare to shed them now.
  You all do know this mantle: I remember
  The first time ever Caesar put it on;
  'Twas on a summer's evening, in his tent,
  That day he overcame the Nervii:
  Look, in this place ran Cassius' dagger through:
  See what a rent the envious Casca made:
  Through this the well-beloved Brutus stabb'd;
  And as he pluck'd his cursed steel away,
  Mark how the blood of Caesar follow'd it,
  As rushing out of doors, to be resolved

If Brutus so unkindly knock'd, or no;
For Brutus, as you know, was Caesar's angel:
Judge, O you gods, how dearly Caesar loved him!
This was the most unkindest cut of all;
For when the noble Caesar saw him stab,
Ingratitude, more strong than traitors' arms,
Quite vanquish'd him: then burst his mighty heart;
And, in his mantle muffling up his face,
Even at the base of Pompey's statua,
Which all the while ran blood, great Caesar fell.
O, what a fall was there, my countrymen!
Then I, and you, and all of us fell down,
Whilst bloody treason flourish'd over us.
O, now you weep; and, I perceive, you feel
The dint of pity: these are gracious drops.
Kind souls, what, weep you when you but behold
Our Caesar's vesture wounded? Look you here,
Here is himself, marr'd, as you see, with traitors.
First Citizen
    O piteous spectacle!
Second Citizen
    O noble Caesar!
Third Citizen
    O woful day!
Fourth Citizen
    O traitors, villains!
First Citizen
    O most bloody sight!
Second Citizen
    We will be revenged.
All
    Revenge! About! Seek! Burn! Fire! Kill! Slay!
    Let not a traitor live!
ANTONY

Stay, countrymen.
First Citizen
Peace there! hear the noble Antony.
Second Citizen
We'll hear him, we'll follow him, we'll die with him.
ANTONY
Good friends, sweet friends, let me not stir you up
To such a sudden flood of mutiny.
They that have done this deed are honourable:
What private griefs they have, alas, I know not,
That made them do it: they are wise and honourable,
And will, no doubt, with reasons answer you.
I come not, friends, to steal away your hearts:
I am no orator, as Brutus is;
But, as you know me all, a plain blunt man,
That love my friend; and that they know full well
That gave me public leave to speak of him:
For I have neither wit, nor words, nor worth,
Action, nor utterance, nor the power of speech,
To stir men's blood: I only speak right on;
I tell you that which you yourselves do know;
Show you sweet Caesar's wounds, poor poor dumb mouths,
And bid them speak for me: but were I Brutus,
And Brutus Antony, there were an Antony
Would ruffle up your spirits and put a tongue
In every wound of Caesar that should move
The stones of Rome to rise and mutiny.
All
We'll mutiny.
First Citizen
We'll burn the house of Brutus.
Third Citizen
Away, then! come, seek the conspirators.

ANTONY
Yet hear me, countrymen; yet hear me speak.
All
Peace, ho! Hear Antony. Most noble Antony!
ANTONY
Why, friends, you go to do you know not what:
Wherein hath Caesar thus deserved your loves?
Alas, you know not: I must tell you then:
You have forgot the will I told you of.
All
Most true. The will! Let's stay and hear the will.
ANTONY
Here is the will, and under Caesar's seal.
To every Roman citizen he gives,
To every several man, seventy-five drachmas.
Second Citizen
Most noble Caesar! We'll revenge his death.
Third Citizen
O royal Caesar!
ANTONY
Hear me with patience.
All
Peace, ho!
ANTONY
Moreover, he hath left you all his walks,
His private arbours and new-planted orchards,
On this side Tiber; he hath left them you,
And to your heirs for ever, common pleasures,
To walk abroad, and recreate yourselves.
Here was a Caesar! when comes such another?
First Citizen
Never, never. Come, away, away!
We'll burn his body in the holy place,
And with the brands fire the traitors' houses.

Take up the body.
Second Citizen
 Go fetch fire.
Third Citizen
 Pluck down benches.
Fourth Citizen
 Pluck down forms, windows, any thing.

Exeunt Citizens with the body

ANTONY
 Now let it work. Mischief, thou art afoot,
 Take thou what course thou wilt!

Enter a Servant

 How now, fellow!
Servant
 Sir, Octavius is already come to Rome.
ANTONY
 Where is he?
Servant
 He and Lepidus are at Caesar's house.
ANTONY
 And thither will I straight to visit him:
 He comes upon a wish. Fortune is merry,
 And in this mood will give us any thing.
Servant
 I heard him say, Brutus and Cassius
 Are rid like madmen through the gates of Rome.
ANTONY
 Belike they had some notice of the people,
 How I had moved them. Bring me to Octavius.

Exeunt

SCENE III.

A street.

Enter CINNA the poet

CINNA THE POET
I dreamt to-night that I did feast with Caesar,
And things unlucky charge my fantasy:
I have no will to wander forth of doors,
Yet something leads me forth.

Enter Citizens

First Citizen
What is your name?
Second Citizen
Whither are you going?
Third Citizen
Where do you dwell?
Fourth Citizen
Are you a married man or a bachelor?
Second Citizen
Answer every man directly.
First Citizen
Ay, and briefly.
Fourth Citizen
Ay, and wisely.
Third Citizen
Ay, and truly, you were best.
CINNA THE POET
What is my name? Whither am I going? Where do I
dwell? Am I a married man or a bachelor? Then, to
answer every man directly and briefly, wisely and
truly: wisely I say, I am a bachelor.
Second Citizen
That's as much as to say, they are fools that marry:

79

you'll bear me a bang for that, I fear. Proceed; directly.
CINNA THE POET
  Directly, I am going to Caesar's funeral.
First Citizen
  As a friend or an enemy?
CINNA THE POET
  As a friend.
Second Citizen
  That matter is answered directly.
Fourth Citizen
  For your dwelling,--briefly.
CINNA THE POET
  Briefly, I dwell by the Capitol.
Third Citizen
  Your name, sir, truly.
CINNA THE POET
  Truly, my name is Cinna.
First Citizen
  Tear him to pieces; he's a conspirator.
CINNA THE POET
  I am Cinna the poet, I am Cinna the poet.
Fourth Citizen
  Tear him for his bad verses, tear him for his bad verses.
CINNA THE POET
  I am not Cinna the conspirator.
Fourth Citizen
  It is no matter, his name's Cinna; pluck but his
  name out of his heart, and turn him going.
Third Citizen
  Tear him, tear him! Come, brands ho! fire-brands:
  to Brutus', to Cassius'; burn all: some to Decius'
  house, and some to Casca's; some to Ligarius': away, go!

Exeunt

ACT IV

SCENE I.

A house in Rome.

ANTONY, OCTAVIUS, and LEPIDUS, seated at a table

ANTONY
 These many, then, shall die; their names are prick'd.
OCTAVIUS
 Your brother too must die; consent you, Lepidus?
LEPIDUS
 I do consent--
OCTAVIUS
 Prick him down, Antony.
LEPIDUS
 Upon condition Publius shall not live,
 Who is your sister's son, Mark Antony.
ANTONY
 He shall not live; look, with a spot I damn him.
 But, Lepidus, go you to Caesar's house;
 Fetch the will hither, and we shall determine
 How to cut off some charge in legacies.
LEPIDUS
 What, shall I find you here?
OCTAVIUS
 Or here, or at the Capitol.

Exit LEPIDUS

ANTONY
 This is a slight unmeritable man,
 Meet to be sent on errands: is it fit,
 The three-fold world divided, he should stand

81

One of the three to share it?
OCTAVIUS
  So you thought him;
  And took his voice who should be prick'd to die,
  In our black sentence and proscription.
ANTONY
  Octavius, I have seen more days than you:
  And though we lay these honours on this man,
  To ease ourselves of divers slanderous loads,
  He shall but bear them as the ass bears gold,
  To groan and sweat under the business,
  Either led or driven, as we point the way;
  And having brought our treasure where we will,
  Then take we down his load, and turn him off,
  Like to the empty ass, to shake his ears,
  And graze in commons.
OCTAVIUS
  You may do your will;
  But he's a tried and valiant soldier.
ANTONY
  So is my horse, Octavius; and for that
  I do appoint him store of provender:
  It is a creature that I teach to fight,
  To wind, to stop, to run directly on,
  His corporal motion govern'd by my spirit.
  And, in some taste, is Lepidus but so;
  He must be taught and train'd and bid go forth;
  A barren-spirited fellow; one that feeds
  On abjects, orts and imitations,
  Which, out of use and staled by other men,
  Begin his fashion: do not talk of him,
  But as a property. And now, Octavius,
  Listen great things:--Brutus and Cassius
  Are levying powers: we must straight make head:

Therefore let our alliance be combined,
Our best friends made, our means stretch'd
And let us presently go sit in council,
How covert matters may be best disclosed,
And open perils surest answered.
OCTAVIUS
Let us do so: for we are at the stake,
And bay'd about with many enemies;
And some that smile have in their hearts, I fear,
Millions of mischiefs.

Exeunt

SCENE II.

Camp near Sardis. Before BRUTUS's tent.

*Drum. Enter BRUTUS, LUCILIUS, LUCIUS, and Soldiers;
TITINIUS and PINDARUS meeting them*

BRUTUS
Stand, ho!
LUCILIUS
Give the word, ho! and stand.
BRUTUS
What now, Lucilius! is Cassius near?
LUCILIUS
He is at hand; and Pindarus is come
To do you salutation from his master.
BRUTUS
He greets me well. Your master, Pindarus,
In his own change, or by ill officers,
Hath given me some worthy cause to wish
Things done, undone: but, if he be at hand,
I shall be satisfied.
PINDARUS

I do not doubt
But that my noble master will appear
Such as he is, full of regard and honour.

BRUTUS

He is not doubted. A word, Lucilius;
How he received you, let me be resolved.

LUCILIUS

With courtesy and with respect enough;
But not with such familiar instances,
Nor with such free and friendly conference,
As he hath used of old.

BRUTUS

Thou hast described
A hot friend cooling: ever note, Lucilius,
When love begins to sicken and decay,
It useth an enforced ceremony.
There are no tricks in plain and simple faith;
But hollow men, like horses hot at hand,
Make gallant show and promise of their mettle;
But when they should endure the bloody spur,
They fall their crests, and, like deceitful jades,
Sink in the trial. Comes his army on?

LUCILIUS

They mean this night in Sardis to be quarter'd;
The greater part, the horse in general,
Are come with Cassius.

BRUTUS

Hark! he is arrived.

Low march within

March gently on to meet him.

Enter CASSIUS and his powers

CASSIUS

Stand, ho!
BRUTUS
Stand, ho! Speak the word along.
First Soldier
Stand!
Second Soldier
Stand!
Third Soldier
Stand!
CASSIUS
Most noble brother, you have done me wrong.
BRUTUS
Judge me, you gods! wrong I mine enemies?
And, if not so, how should I wrong a brother?
CASSIUS
Brutus, this sober form of yours hides wrongs;
And when you do them--
BRUTUS
Cassius, be content.
Speak your griefs softly: I do know you well.
Before the eyes of both our armies here,
Which should perceive nothing but love from us,
Let us not wrangle: bid them move away;
Then in my tent, Cassius, enlarge your griefs,
And I will give you audience.
CASSIUS
Pindarus,
Bid our commanders lead their charges off
A little from this ground.
BRUTUS
Lucilius, do you the like; and let no man
Come to our tent till we have done our conference.
Let Lucius and Titinius guard our door.

Exeunt

85

SCENE III.

Brutus's tent.

Enter BRUTUS and CASSIUS

CASSIUS
That you have wrong'd me doth appear in this:
You have condemn'd and noted Lucius Pella
For taking bribes here of the Sardians;
Wherein my letters, praying on his side,
Because I knew the man, were slighted off.
BRUTUS
You wronged yourself to write in such a case.
CASSIUS
In such a time as this it is not meet
That every nice offence should bear his comment.
BRUTUS
Let me tell you, Cassius, you yourself
Are much condemn'd to have an itching palm;
To sell and mart your offices for gold
To undeservers.
CASSIUS
I an itching palm!
You know that you are Brutus that speak this,
Or, by the gods, this speech were else your last.
BRUTUS
The name of Cassius honours this corruption,
And chastisement doth therefore hide his head.
CASSIUS
Chastisement!
BRUTUS
Remember March, the ides of March remember:
Did not great Julius bleed for justice' sake?

What villain touch'd his body, that did stab,
And not for justice? What, shall one of us
That struck the foremost man of all this world
But for supporting robbers, shall we now
Contaminate our fingers with base bribes,
And sell the mighty space of our large honours
For so much trash as may be grasped thus?
I had rather be a dog, and bay the moon,
Than such a Roman.

CASSIUS
Brutus, bay not me;
I'll not endure it: you forget yourself,
To hedge me in; I am a soldier, I,
Older in practise, abler than yourself
To make conditions.

BRUTUS
Go to; you are not, Cassius.

CASSIUS
I am.

BRUTUS
I say you are not.

CASSIUS
Urge me no more, I shall forget myself;
Have mind upon your health, tempt me no further.

BRUTUS
Away, slight man!

CASSIUS
Is't possible?

BRUTUS
Hear me, for I will speak.
Must I give way and room to your rash choler?
Shall I be frighted when a madman stares?

CASSIUS
O ye gods, ye gods! must I endure all this?

BRUTUS
All this! ay, more: fret till your proud heart break;
Go show your slaves how choleric you are,
And make your bondmen tremble. Must I budge?
Must I observe you? must I stand and crouch
Under your testy humour? By the gods
You shall digest the venom of your spleen,
Though it do split you; for, from this day forth,
I'll use you for my mirth, yea, for my laughter,
When you are waspish.
CASSIUS
Is it come to this?
BRUTUS
You say you are a better soldier:
Let it appear so; make your vaunting true,
And it shall please me well: for mine own part,
I shall be glad to learn of noble men.
CASSIUS
You wrong me every way; you wrong me, Brutus;
I said, an elder soldier, not a better:
Did I say 'better'?
BRUTUS
If you did, I care not.
CASSIUS
When Caesar lived, he durst not thus have moved me.
BRUTUS
Peace, peace! you durst not so have tempted him.
CASSIUS
I durst not!
BRUTUS
No.
CASSIUS
What, durst not tempt him!
BRUTUS

For your life you durst not!
CASSIUS
    Do not presume too much upon my love;
    I may do that I shall be sorry for.
BRUTUS
    You have done that you should be sorry for.
    There is no terror, Cassius, in your threats,
    For I am arm'd so strong in honesty
    That they pass by me as the idle wind,
    Which I respect not. I did send to you
    For certain sums of gold, which you denied me:
    For I can raise no money by vile means:
    By heaven, I had rather coin my heart,
    And drop my blood for drachmas, than to wring
    From the hard hands of peasants their vile trash
    By any indirection: I did send
    To you for gold to pay my legions,
    Which you denied me: was that done like Cassius?
    Should I have answer'd Caius Cassius so?
    When Marcus Brutus grows so covetous,
    To lock such rascal counters from his friends,
    Be ready, gods, with all your thunderbolts;
    Dash him to pieces!
CASSIUS
    I denied you not.
BRUTUS
    You did.
CASSIUS
    I did not: he was but a fool that brought
    My answer back. Brutus hath rived my heart:
    A friend should bear his friend's infirmities,
    But Brutus makes mine greater than they are.
BRUTUS
    I do not, till you practise them on me.

CASSIUS
You love me not.
BRUTUS
I do not like your faults.
CASSIUS
A friendly eye could never see such faults.
BRUTUS
A flatterer's would not, though they do appear
As huge as high Olympus.
CASSIUS
Come, Antony, and young Octavius, come,
Revenge yourselves alone on Cassius,
For Cassius is aweary of the world;
Hated by one he loves; braved by his brother;
Cheque'd like a bondman; all his faults observed,
Set in a note-book, learn'd, and conn'd by rote,
To cast into my teeth. O, I could weep
My spirit from mine eyes! There is my dagger,
And here my naked breast; within, a heart
Dearer than Plutus' mine, richer than gold:
If that thou be'st a Roman, take it forth;
I, that denied thee gold, will give my heart:
Strike, as thou didst at Caesar; for, I know,
When thou didst hate him worst, thou lovedst him better
Than ever thou lovedst Cassius.
BRUTUS
Sheathe your dagger:
Be angry when you will, it shall have scope;
Do what you will, dishonour shall be humour.
O Cassius, you are yoked with a lamb
That carries anger as the flint bears fire;
Who, much enforced, shows a hasty spark,
And straight is cold again.
CASSIUS

Hath Cassius lived
To be but mirth and laughter to his Brutus,
When grief, and blood ill-temper'd, vexeth him?
BRUTUS
When I spoke that, I was ill-temper'd too.
CASSIUS
Do you confess so much? Give me your hand.
BRUTUS
And my heart too.
CASSIUS
O Brutus!
BRUTUS
What's the matter?
CASSIUS
Have not you love enough to bear with me,
When that rash humour which my mother gave me
Makes me forgetful?
BRUTUS
Yes, Cassius; and, from henceforth,
When you are over-earnest with your Brutus,
He'll think your mother chides, and leave you so.
Poet
[Within] Let me go in to see the generals;
There is some grudge between 'em, 'tis not meet
They be alone.
LUCILIUS
[Within] You shall not come to them.
Poet
[Within] Nothing but death shall stay me.

Enter Poet, followed by LUCILIUS, TITINIUS, and LUCIUS

CASSIUS
How now! what's the matter?
Poet

For shame, you generals! what do you mean?
Love, and be friends, as two such men should be;
For I have seen more years, I'm sure, than ye.
CASSIUS
Ha, ha! how vilely doth this cynic rhyme!
BRUTUS
Get you hence, sirrah; saucy fellow, hence!
CASSIUS
Bear with him, Brutus; 'tis his fashion.
BRUTUS
I'll know his humour, when he knows his time:
What should the wars do with these jigging fools?
Companion, hence!
CASSIUS
Away, away, be gone.

Exit Poet

BRUTUS
Lucilius and Titinius, bid the commanders
Prepare to lodge their companies to-night.
CASSIUS
And come yourselves, and bring Messala with you
Immediately to us.

Exeunt LUCILIUS and TITINIUS

BRUTUS
Lucius, a bowl of wine!

Exit LUCIUS

CASSIUS
I did not think you could have been so angry.
BRUTUS
O Cassius, I am sick of many griefs.

CASSIUS
Of your philosophy you make no use,
If you give place to accidental evils.
BRUTUS
No man bears sorrow better. Portia is dead.
CASSIUS
Ha! Portia!
BRUTUS
She is dead.
CASSIUS
How 'scaped I killing when I cross'd you so?
O insupportable and touching loss!
Upon what sickness?
BRUTUS
Impatient of my absence,
And grief that young Octavius with Mark Antony
Have made themselves so strong:--for with her death
That tidings came;--with this she fell distract,
And, her attendants absent, swallow'd fire.
CASSIUS
And died so?
BRUTUS
Even so.
CASSIUS
O ye immortal gods!

Re-enter LUCIUS, with wine and taper

BRUTUS
Speak no more of her. Give me a bowl of wine.
In this I bury all unkindness, Cassius.
CASSIUS
My heart is thirsty for that noble pledge.
Fill, Lucius, till the wine o'erswell the cup;
I cannot drink too much of Brutus' love.

BRUTUS
Come in, Titinius!

Exit LUCIUS

Re-enter TITINIUS, with MESSALA

Welcome, good Messala.
Now sit we close about this taper here,
And call in question our necessities.
CASSIUS
Portia, art thou gone?
BRUTUS
No more, I pray you.
Messala, I have here received letters,
That young Octavius and Mark Antony
Come down upon us with a mighty power,
Bending their expedition toward Philippi.
MESSALA
Myself have letters of the selfsame tenor.
BRUTUS
With what addition?
MESSALA
That by proscription and bills of outlawry,
Octavius, Antony, and Lepidus,
Have put to death an hundred senators.
BRUTUS
Therein our letters do not well agree;
Mine speak of seventy senators that died
By their proscriptions, Cicero being one.
CASSIUS
Cicero one!
MESSALA
Cicero is dead,

And by that order of proscription.
Had you your letters from your wife, my lord?
BRUTUS
No, Messala.
MESSALA
Nor nothing in your letters writ of her?
BRUTUS
Nothing, Messala.
MESSALA
That, methinks, is strange.
BRUTUS
Why ask you? hear you aught of her in yours?
MESSALA
No, my lord.
BRUTUS
Now, as you are a Roman, tell me true.
MESSALA
Then like a Roman bear the truth I tell:
For certain she is dead, and by strange manner.
BRUTUS
Why, farewell, Portia. We must die, Messala:
With meditating that she must die once,
I have the patience to endure it now.
MESSALA
Even so great men great losses should endure.
CASSIUS
I have as much of this in art as you,
But yet my nature could not bear it so.
BRUTUS
Well, to our work alive. What do you think
Of marching to Philippi presently?
CASSIUS
I do not think it good.
BRUTUS

Your reason?

CASSIUS

This it is:

'Tis better that the enemy seek us:

So shall he waste his means, weary his soldiers,

Doing himself offence; whilst we, lying still,

Are full of rest, defense, and nimbleness.

BRUTUS

Good reasons must, of force, give place to better.

The people 'twixt Philippi and this ground

Do stand but in a forced affection;

For they have grudged us contribution:

The enemy, marching along by them,

By them shall make a fuller number up,

Come on refresh'd, new-added, and encouraged;

From which advantage shall we cut him off,

If at Philippi we do face him there,

These people at our back.

CASSIUS

Hear me, good brother.

BRUTUS

Under your pardon. You must note beside,

That we have tried the utmost of our friends,

Our legions are brim-full, our cause is ripe:

The enemy increaseth every day;

We, at the height, are ready to decline.

There is a tide in the affairs of men,

Which, taken at the flood, leads on to fortune;

Omitted, all the voyage of their life

Is bound in shallows and in miseries.

On such a full sea are we now afloat;

And we must take the current when it serves,

Or lose our ventures.

CASSIUS

Then, with your will, go on;
We'll along ourselves, and meet them at Philippi.
BRUTUS
The deep of night is crept upon our talk,
And nature must obey necessity;
Which we will niggard with a little rest.
There is no more to say?
CASSIUS
No more. Good night:
Early to-morrow will we rise, and hence.
BRUTUS
Lucius!

Enter LUCIUS

My gown.

Exit LUCIUS

Farewell, good Messala:
Good night, Titinius. Noble, noble Cassius,
Good night, and good repose.
CASSIUS
O my dear brother!
This was an ill beginning of the night:
Never come such division 'tween our souls!
Let it not, Brutus.
BRUTUS
Every thing is well.
CASSIUS
Good night, my lord.
BRUTUS
Good night, good brother.
TITINIUS and MESSALA
Good night, Lord Brutus.

BRUTUS
Farewell, every one.

Exeunt all but BRUTUS

Re-enter LUCIUS, with the gown

Give me the gown. Where is thy instrument?
LUCIUS
Here in the tent.
BRUTUS
What, thou speak'st drowsily?
Poor knave, I blame thee not; thou art o'er-watch'd.
Call Claudius and some other of my men:
I'll have them sleep on cushions in my tent.
LUCIUS
Varro and Claudius!

Enter VARRO and CLAUDIUS

VARRO
Calls my lord?
BRUTUS
I pray you, sirs, lie in my tent and sleep;
It may be I shall raise you by and by
On business to my brother Cassius.
VARRO
So please you, we will stand and watch your pleasure.
BRUTUS
I will not have it so: lie down, good sirs;
It may be I shall otherwise bethink me.
Look, Lucius, here's the book I sought for so;
I put it in the pocket of my gown.

VARRO and CLAUDIUS lie down

LUCIUS
I was sure your lordship did not give it me.
BRUTUS
Bear with me, good boy, I am much forgetful.
Canst thou hold up thy heavy eyes awhile,
And touch thy instrument a strain or two?
LUCIUS
Ay, my lord, an't please you.
BRUTUS
It does, my boy:
I trouble thee too much, but thou art willing.
LUCIUS
It is my duty, sir.
BRUTUS
I should not urge thy duty past thy might;
I know young bloods look for a time of rest.
LUCIUS
I have slept, my lord, already.
BRUTUS
It was well done; and thou shalt sleep again;
I will not hold thee long: if I do live,
I will be good to thee.

Music, and a song

This is a sleepy tune. O murderous slumber,
Lay'st thou thy leaden mace upon my boy,
That plays thee music? Gentle knave, good night;
I will not do thee so much wrong to wake thee:
If thou dost nod, thou break'st thy instrument;
I'll take it from thee; and, good boy, good night.
Let me see, let me see; is not the leaf turn'd down
Where I left reading? Here it is, I think.

Enter the Ghost of CAESAR

How ill this taper burns! Ha! who comes here?
I think it is the weakness of mine eyes
That shapes this monstrous apparition.
It comes upon me. Art thou any thing?
Art thou some god, some angel, or some devil,
That makest my blood cold and my hair to stare?
Speak to me what thou art.

GHOST
Thy evil spirit, Brutus.

BRUTUS
Why comest thou?

GHOST
To tell thee thou shalt see me at Philippi.

BRUTUS
Well; then I shall see thee again?

GHOST
Ay, at Philippi.

BRUTUS
Why, I will see thee at Philippi, then.

Exit Ghost

Now I have taken heart thou vanishest:
Ill spirit, I would hold more talk with thee.
Boy, Lucius! Varro! Claudius! Sirs, awake! Claudius!

LUCIUS
The strings, my lord, are false.

BRUTUS
He thinks he still is at his instrument.
Lucius, awake!

LUCIUS
My lord?

BRUTUS
Didst thou dream, Lucius, that thou so criedst out?

LUCIUS
  My lord, I do not know that I did cry.
BRUTUS
  Yes, that thou didst: didst thou see any thing?
LUCIUS
  Nothing, my lord.
BRUTUS
  Sleep again, Lucius. Sirrah Claudius!

To VARRO

  Fellow thou, awake!
VARRO
  My lord?
CLAUDIUS
  My lord?
BRUTUS
  Why did you so cry out, sirs, in your sleep?
VARRO and CLAUDIUS
  Did we, my lord?
BRUTUS
  Ay: saw you any thing?
VARRO
  No, my lord, I saw nothing.
CLAUDIUS
  Nor I, my lord.
BRUTUS
  Go and commend me to my brother Cassius;
  Bid him set on his powers betimes before,
  And we will follow.
VARRO and CLAUDIUS
  It shall be done, my lord.

Exeunt

ACT V

SCENE I.

The plains of Philippi.

Enter OCTAVIUS, ANTONY, and their army

OCTAVIUS

Now, Antony, our hopes are answered:
You said the enemy would not come down,
But keep the hills and upper regions;
It proves not so: their battles are at hand;
They mean to warn us at Philippi here,
Answering before we do demand of them.

ANTONY

Tut, I am in their bosoms, and I know
Wherefore they do it: they could be content
To visit other places; and come down
With fearful bravery, thinking by this face
To fasten in our thoughts that they have courage;
But 'tis not so.

Enter a Messenger

Messenger

Prepare you, generals:
The enemy comes on in gallant show;
Their bloody sign of battle is hung out,
And something to be done immediately.

ANTONY

Octavius, lead your battle softly on,
Upon the left hand of the even field.

OCTAVIUS

Upon the right hand I; keep thou the left.

ANTONY
Why do you cross me in this exigent?
OCTAVIUS
I do not cross you; but I will do so.

March

Drum. Enter BRUTUS, CASSIUS, and their Army;
LUCILIUS, TITINIUS, MESSALA, and others

BRUTUS
They stand, and would have parley.
CASSIUS
Stand fast, Titinius: we must out and talk.
OCTAVIUS
Mark Antony, shall we give sign of battle?
ANTONY
No, Caesar, we will answer on their charge.
Make forth; the generals would have some words.
OCTAVIUS
Stir not until the signal.
BRUTUS
Words before blows: is it so, countrymen?
OCTAVIUS
Not that we love words better, as you do.
BRUTUS
Good words are better than bad strokes, Octavius.
ANTONY
In your bad strokes, Brutus, you give good words:
Witness the hole you made in Caesar's heart,
Crying 'Long live! hail, Caesar!'
CASSIUS
Antony,
The posture of your blows are yet unknown;

But for your words, they rob the Hybla bees,
And leave them honeyless.
ANTONY
Not stingless too.
BRUTUS
O, yes, and soundless too;
For you have stol'n their buzzing, Antony,
And very wisely threat before you sting.
ANTONY
Villains, you did not so, when your vile daggers
Hack'd one another in the sides of Caesar:
You show'd your teeth like apes, and fawn'd like
hounds,
And bow'd like bondmen, kissing Caesar's feet;
Whilst damned Casca, like a cur, behind
Struck Caesar on the neck. O you flatterers!
CASSIUS
Flatterers! Now, Brutus, thank yourself:
This tongue had not offended so to-day,
If Cassius might have ruled.
OCTAVIUS
Come, come, the cause: if arguing make us sweat,
The proof of it will turn to redder drops. Look;
I draw a sword against conspirators;
When think you that the sword goes up again?
Never, till Caesar's three and thirty wounds
Be well avenged; or till another Caesar
Have added slaughter to the sword of traitors.
BRUTUS
Caesar, thou canst not die by traitors' hands,
Unless thou bring'st them with thee.
OCTAVIUS
So I hope;
I was not born to die on Brutus' sword.

BRUTUS
O, if thou wert the noblest of thy strain,
Young man, thou couldst not die more honourable.
CASSIUS
A peevish schoolboy, worthless of such honour,
Join'd with a masker and a reveller!
ANTONY
Old Cassius still!
OCTAVIUS
Come, Antony, away!
Defiance, traitors, hurl we in your teeth:
If you dare fight to-day, come to the field;
If not, when you have stomachs.

Exeunt OCTAVIUS, ANTONY, and their army

CASSIUS
Why, now, blow wind, swell billow and swim bark!
The storm is up, and all is on the hazard.
BRUTUS
Ho, Lucilius! hark, a word with you.
LUCILIUS
[Standing forth]   My lord?

BRUTUS and LUCILIUS converse apart

CASSIUS
Messala!
MESSALA
[Standing forth] What says my general?
CASSIUS
Messala,
This is my birth-day; as this very day
Was Cassius born. Give me thy hand, Messala:
Be thou my witness that against my will,

As Pompey was, am I compell'd to set
Upon one battle all our liberties.
You know that I held Epicurus strong
And his opinion: now I change my mind,
And partly credit things that do presage.
Coming from Sardis, on our former ensign
Two mighty eagles fell, and there they perch'd,
Gorging and feeding from our soldiers' hands;
Who to Philippi here consorted us:
This morning are they fled away and gone;
And in their steads do ravens, crows and kites,
Fly o'er our heads and downward look on us,
As we were sickly prey: their shadows seem
A canopy most fatal, under which
Our army lies, ready to give up the ghost.
MESSALA
Believe not so.
CASSIUS
I but believe it partly;
For I am fresh of spirit and resolved
To meet all perils very constantly.
BRUTUS
Even so, Lucilius.
CASSIUS
Now, most noble Brutus,
The gods to-day stand friendly, that we may,
Lovers in peace, lead on our days to age!
But since the affairs of men rest still incertain,
Let's reason with the worst that may befall.
If we do lose this battle, then is this
The very last time we shall speak together:
What are you then determined to do?
BRUTUS
Even by the rule of that philosophy

By which I did blame Cato for the death
Which he did give himself, I know not how,
But I do find it cowardly and vile,
For fear of what might fall, so to prevent
The time of life: arming myself with patience
To stay the providence of some high powers
That govern us below.
CASSIUS
Then, if we lose this battle,
You are contented to be led in triumph
Thorough the streets of Rome?
BRUTUS
No, Cassius, no: think not, thou noble Roman,
That ever Brutus will go bound to Rome;
He bears too great a mind. But this same day
Must end that work the ides of March begun;
And whether we shall meet again I know not.
Therefore our everlasting farewell take:
For ever, and for ever, farewell, Cassius!
If we do meet again, why, we shall smile;
If not, why then, this parting was well made.
CASSIUS
For ever, and for ever, farewell, Brutus!
If we do meet again, we'll smile indeed;
If not, 'tis true this parting was well made.
BRUTUS
Why, then, lead on. O, that a man might know
The end of this day's business ere it come!
But it sufficeth that the day will end,
And then the end is known. Come, ho! away!

Exeunt

SCENE II.

The same. The field of battle.

Alarum. Enter BRUTUS and MESSALA

BRUTUS
Ride, ride, Messala, ride, and give these bills
Unto the legions on the other side.

Loud alarum

Let them set on at once; for I perceive
But cold demeanor in Octavius' wing,
And sudden push gives them the overthrow.
Ride, ride, Messala: let them all come down.

Exeunt

SCENE III.

Another part of the field.

Alarums. Enter CASSIUS and TITINIUS

CASSIUS
O, look, Titinius, look, the villains fly!
Myself have to mine own turn'd enemy:
This ensign here of mine was turning back;
I slew the coward, and did take it from him.
TITINIUS
O Cassius, Brutus gave the word too early;
Who, having some advantage on Octavius,
Took it too eagerly: his soldiers fell to spoil,
Whilst we by Antony are all enclosed.

Enter PINDARUS

PINDARUS

Fly further off, my lord, fly further off;
Mark Antony is in your tents, my lord
Fly, therefore, noble Cassius, fly far off.
CASSIUS
This hill is far enough. Look, look, Titinius;
Are those my tents where I perceive the fire?
TITINIUS
They are, my lord.
CASSIUS
Titinius, if thou lovest me,
Mount thou my horse, and hide thy spurs in him,
Till he have brought thee up to yonder troops,
And here again; that I may rest assured
Whether yond troops are friend or enemy.
TITINIUS
I will be here again, even with a thought.

Exit

CASSIUS
Go, Pindarus, get higher on that hill;
My sight was ever thick; regard Titinius,
And tell me what thou notest about the field.

PINDARUS ascends the hill

This day I breathed first: time is come round,
And where I did begin, there shall I end;
My life is run his compass. Sirrah, what news?
PINDARUS
[Above] O my lord!
CASSIUS
What news?
PINDARUS
[Above] Titinius is enclosed round about

With horsemen, that make to him on the spur;
Yet he spurs on. Now they are almost on him.
Now, Titinius! Now some light. O, he lights too.
He's ta'en.

Shout

And, hark! they shout for joy.
CASSIUS
Come down, behold no more.
O, coward that I am, to live so long,
To see my best friend ta'en before my face!

PINDARUS descends

Come hither, sirrah:
In Parthia did I take thee prisoner;
And then I swore thee, saving of thy life,
That whatsoever I did bid thee do,
Thou shouldst attempt it. Come now, keep thine oath;
Now be a freeman: and with this good sword,
That ran through Caesar's bowels, search this bosom.
Stand not to answer: here, take thou the hilts;
And, when my face is cover'd, as 'tis now,
Guide thou the sword.

PINDARUS stabs him

Caesar, thou art revenged,
Even with the sword that kill'd thee.

Dies

PINDARUS
So, I am free; yet would not so have been,
Durst I have done my will. O Cassius,
Far from this country Pindarus shall run,

Where never Roman shall take note of him.

Exit

Re-enter TITINIUS with MESSALA

MESSALA
  It is but change, Titinius; for Octavius
  Is overthrown by noble Brutus' power,
  As Cassius' legions are by Antony.
TITINIUS
  These tidings will well comfort Cassius.
MESSALA
  Where did you leave him?
TITINIUS
  All disconsolate,
  With Pindarus his bondman, on this hill.
MESSALA
  Is not that he t hat lies upon the ground?
TITINIUS
  He lies not like the living. O my heart!
MESSALA
  Is not that he?
TITINIUS
  No, this was he, Messala,
  But Cassius is no more. O setting sun,
  As in thy red rays thou dost sink to-night,
  So in his red blood Cassius' day is set;
  The sun of Rome is set! Our day is gone;
  Clouds, dews, and dangers come; our deeds are done!
  Mistrust of my success hath done this deed.
MESSALA
  Mistrust of good success hath done this deed.
  O hateful error, melancholy's child,

Why dost thou show to the apt thoughts of men
The things that are not? O error, soon conceived,
Thou never comest unto a happy birth,
But kill'st the mother that engender'd thee!
TITINIUS
What, Pindarus! where art thou, Pindarus?
MESSALA
Seek him, Titinius, whilst I go to meet
The noble Brutus, thrusting this report
Into his ears; I may say, thrusting it;
For piercing steel and darts envenomed
Shall be as welcome to the ears of Brutus
As tidings of this sight.
TITINIUS
Hie you, Messala,
And I will seek for Pindarus the while.

Exit MESSALA

Why didst thou send me forth, brave Cassius?
Did I not meet thy friends? and did not they
Put on my brows this wreath of victory,
And bid me give it thee? Didst thou not hear their
shouts?
Alas, thou hast misconstrued every thing!
But, hold thee, take this garland on thy brow;
Thy Brutus bid me give it thee, and I
Will do his bidding. Brutus, come apace,
And see how I regarded Caius Cassius.
By your leave, gods:--this is a Roman's part
Come, Cassius' sword, and find Titinius' heart.

Kills himself

Alarum. Re-enter MESSALA, with BRUTUS, CATO,
STRATO, VOLUMNIUS, and LUCILIUS

BRUTUS
Where, where, Messala, doth his body lie?
MESSALA
Lo, yonder, and Titinius mourning it.
BRUTUS
Titinius' face is upward.
CATO
He is slain.
BRUTUS
O Julius Caesar, thou art mighty yet!
Thy spirit walks abroad and turns our swords
In our own proper entrails.

Low alarums

CATO
Brave Titinius!
Look, whether he have not crown'd dead Cassius!
BRUTUS
Are yet two Romans living such as these?
The last of all the Romans, fare thee well!
It is impossible that ever Rome
Should breed thy fellow. Friends, I owe more tears
To this dead man than you shall see me pay.
I shall find time, Cassius, I shall find time.
Come, therefore, and to Thasos send his body:
His funerals shall not be in our camp,
Lest it discomfort us. Lucilius, come;
And come, young Cato; let us to the field.
Labeo and Flavius, set our battles on:
'Tis three o'clock; and, Romans, yet ere night
We shall try fortune in a second fight.

Exeunt

SCENE IV.

Another part of the field.

Alarum. Enter fighting, Soldiers of both armies; then
BRUTUS, CATO, LUCILIUS, and others

BRUTUS
Yet, countrymen, O, yet hold up your heads!
CATO
What bastard doth not? Who will go with me?
I will proclaim my name about the field:
I am the son of Marcus Cato, ho!
A foe to tyrants, and my country's friend;
I am the son of Marcus Cato, ho!
BRUTUS
And I am Brutus, Marcus Brutus, I;
Brutus, my country's friend; know me for Brutus!

Exit

LUCILIUS
O young and noble Cato, art thou down?
Why, now thou diest as bravely as Titinius;
And mayst be honour'd, being Cato's son.
First Soldier
Yield, or thou diest.
LUCILIUS
Only I yield to die:
There is so much that thou wilt kill me straight;

Offering money

Kill Brutus, and be honour'd in his death.
First Soldier
We must not. A noble prisoner!

Second Soldier
    Room, ho! Tell Antony, Brutus is ta'en.
First Soldier
    I'll tell the news. Here comes the general.

Enter ANTONY

    Brutus is ta'en, Brutus is ta'en, my lord.
ANTONY
    Where is he?
LUCILIUS
    Safe, Antony; Brutus is safe enough:
    I dare assure thee that no enemy
    Shall ever take alive the noble Brutus:
    The gods defend him from so great a shame!
    When you do find him, or alive or dead,
    He will be found like Brutus, like himself.
ANTONY
    This is not Brutus, friend; but, I assure you,
    A prize no less in worth: keep this man safe;
    Give him all kindness: I had rather have
    Such men my friends than enemies. Go on,
    And see whether Brutus be alive or dead;
    And bring us word unto Octavius' tent
    How every thing is chanced.

Exeunt

SCENE V.

Another part of the field.

*Enter BRUTUS, DARDANIUS, CLITUS, STRATO, and
VOLUMNIUS*

BRUTUS
    Come, poor remains of friends, rest on this rock.

CLITUS
Statilius show'd the torch-light, but, my lord,
He came not back: he is or ta'en or slain.
BRUTUS
Sit thee down, Clitus: slaying is the word;
It is a deed in fashion. Hark thee, Clitus.

Whispers

CLITUS
What, I, my lord? No, not for all the world.
BRUTUS
Peace then! no words.
CLITUS
I'll rather kill myself.
BRUTUS
Hark thee, Dardanius.

Whispers

DARDANIUS
Shall I do such a deed?
CLITUS
O Dardanius!
DARDANIUS
O Clitus!
CLITUS
What ill request did Brutus make to thee?
DARDANIUS
To kill him, Clitus. Look, he meditates.
CLITUS
Now is that noble vessel full of grief,
That it runs over even at his eyes.
BRUTUS
Come hither, good Volumnius; list a word.

VOLUMNIUS
  What says my lord?
BRUTUS
  Why, this, Volumnius:
  The ghost of Caesar hath appear'd to me
  Two several times by night; at Sardis once,
  And, this last night, here in Philippi fields:
  I know my hour is come.
VOLUMNIUS
  Not so, my lord.
BRUTUS
  Nay, I am sure it is, Volumnius.
  Thou seest the world, Volumnius, how it goes;
  Our enemies have beat us to the pit:

Low alarums

  It is more worthy to leap in ourselves,
  Than tarry till they push us. Good Volumnius,
  Thou know'st that we two went to school together:
  Even for that our love of old, I prithee,
  Hold thou my sword-hilts, whilst I run on it.
VOLUMNIUS
  That's not an office for a friend, my lord.

Alarum still

CLITUS
  Fly, fly, my lord; there is no tarrying here.
BRUTUS
  Farewell to you; and you; and you, Volumnius.
  Strato, thou hast been all this while asleep;
  Farewell to thee too, Strato. Countrymen,
  My heart doth joy that yet in all my life
  I found no man but he was true to me.

I shall have glory by this losing day
More than Octavius and Mark Antony
By this vile conquest shall attain unto.
So fare you well at once; for Brutus' tongue
Hath almost ended his life's history:
Night hangs upon mine eyes; my bones would rest,
That have but labour'd to attain this hour.

Alarum. Cry within, 'Fly, fly, fly!'

CLITUS
  Fly, my lord, fly.
BRUTUS
  Hence! I will follow.

Exeunt CLITUS, DARDANIUS, and VOLUMNIUS

I prithee, Strato, stay thou by thy lord:
Thou art a fellow of a good respect;
Thy life hath had some smatch of honour in it:
Hold then my sword, and turn away thy face,
While I do run upon it. Wilt thou, Strato?
STRATO
  Give me your hand first. Fare you well, my lord.
BRUTUS
  Farewell, good Strato.

Runs on his sword

Caesar, now be still:
I kill'd not thee with half so good a will.

Dies

*Alarum. Retreat. Enter OCTAVIUS, ANTONY, MESSALA,
LUCILIUS, and the army*

OCTAVIUS
    What man is that?
MESSALA
    My master's man. Strato, where is thy master?
STRATO
    Free from the bondage you are in, Messala:
    The conquerors can but make a fire of him;
    For Brutus only overcame himself,
    And no man else hath honour by his death.
LUCILIUS
    So Brutus should be found. I thank thee, Brutus,
    That thou hast proved Lucilius' saying true.
OCTAVIUS
    All that served Brutus, I will entertain them.
    Fellow, wilt thou bestow thy time with me?
STRATO
    Ay, if Messala will prefer me to you.
OCTAVIUS
    Do so, good Messala.
MESSALA
    How died my master, Strato?
STRATO
    I held the sword, and he did run on it.
MESSALA
    Octavius, then take him to follow thee,
    That did the latest service to my master.
ANTONY
    This was the noblest Roman of them all:
    All the conspirators save only he
    Did that they did in envy of great Caesar;
    He only, in a general honest thought
    And common good to all, made one of them.
    His life was gentle, and the elements

So mix'd in him that Nature might stand up
And say to all the world 'This was a man!'
OCTAVIUS
According to his virtue let us use him,
With all respect and rites of burial.
Within my tent his bones to-night shall lie,
Most like a soldier, order'd honourably.
So call the field to rest; and let's away,
To part the glories of this happy day.

Exeunt

Biography

A Short Life of Edward de Vere, 17th Earl of Oxford

by Dr. Kevin Gilvary, President
The de Vere Society

He was born on 12 April 1550 at Castle Hedingham, his family's ancestral home. His father, John de Vere, 16th Earl, was Lord Great Chamberlain and attended the coronations of both Mary and Elizabeth Tudor. His mother was Margaret Golding. Edward was 11 when, in 1561, Queen Elizabeth visited Hedingham for four days of masques, feasting and entertainments. When his father died in 1562, young Oxford left to become, like Bertram in *All's Well that Ends Well*, a ward of the Crown under the guardianship of William Cecil, the Queen's private secretary (later Lord Burghley, Lord Treasurer). His mother married Charles Tyrrell and seems to have passed out of the boy's life. His sister Mary went to live with her stepfather and the siblings were not reunited for some years.

According to a curriculum in Cecil's own hand, Edward de Vere's daily studies included dancing, French, Latin, writing and drawing, cosmography, penmanship, riding, shooting, exercise and prayer. Edward de Vere showed a prodigious talent for scholarship from his early years, and we may ascribe his lifelong love of learning to the influence of two of his early tutors. The first was Sir Thomas Smith who was, perhaps, England's most respected Greek scholar and the former Cambridge tutor of Sir William Cecil. It was, no doubt, through Cecil's influence that Edward de Vere spent some time living in the household of Smith in his early years, during which time he spent about five months at Smith's alma mater, Queens' College, Cambridge. Smith was a scholar of widely varied interests – this was reflected in his 400-volume library, some of which is still extant at Cambridge. De Vere's other tutor was Laurence Nowell, who was not only an accomplished cartographer but was also England's premier scholar of Anglo-Saxon literature – it was Nowell who possessed the only known copy of *Beowulf*.

Another important influence on Edward de Vere's early studies was his maternal uncle Arthur Golding, an officer in the Court of Wards under Cecil, who is credited with the translation of Ovid's *Metamorphoses*, published in 1567, a book widely recognised as having a major influence on 'Shakespeare'.

Following on from his matriculation at Cambridge in November 1558, Edward was awarded an honorary MA by Cambridge during a Royal progress in August 1564, and another degree by Oxford University during a Royal progress in 1566. Edward de Vere then attended Gray's Inn to study law. One notable feature of the Elizabethan Inns of Court was a tradition of mounting dramatic productions and of hosting the various touring companies of players.

In 1570 he served in a military campaign in Scotland under the Earl of Sussex. By 1571, he was reported as a leading luminary of the Court and, for a time, a favourite of Queen Elizabeth. In December 1571 he married Anne Cecil, aged 15, daughter of his guardian. This was a dynastic marriage where all the advantage accrued to Cecil who, ennobled as Baron Burghley, had reduced the social gap between himself and the young Earl.

While Oxford was away on a Grand Tour of Europe, he heard that his daughter Elizabeth Vere had been born in July 1575. On his return in early 1576, he appeared to have been convinced that Elizabeth was not his child; consequently he became estranged from Anne for five years, and exiled himself from Court, taking up residence in the Savoy and concerning himself with literary and musical patronage.

Already, in 1573, *Cardanus Comfort* (the Consolations of Boethius) had been translated from Latin by Thomas Bedingfield and dedicated to Oxford; and published with a preface written by him. In 1576 an anthology, *A Paradise of Daintie Devices*, including several poems by Oxford, was published. These are juvenile works but already show affinities, in both style and thought, with those of the mature Shakespeare.

Oxford's Grand Tour had taken in Paris, Strasbourg, Venice, Genoa, Florence, Palermo and, on his way back through France, Rousillon – the setting for *Love's Labour's Lost*. Oxford spent the best part of a year travelling in Italy in 1576, and becoming involved with moneylenders. He came back to England fluent in Italian and well acquainted with the northern Italian cities, to be satirised by Gabriel Harvey as 'The Italian Earl'. On his way back his ship was attacked by pirates in the English Channel (cf. *Hamlet*). Fourteen of 'Shakespeare's' plays have Italian settings, in which he put his detailed knowledge of the country, beyond pure book knowledge, to good use.

1573 saw the birth of Henry Wriothesley, Earl of Southampton. Although history has not bequeathed to us any evidence of a direct relationship between the two men, in the relatively small world of the royal Court, they must have been acquainted with each other. The poems *Venus and Adonis* (1593) and *The Rape of Lucrece* (1594) were dedicated to Southampton. These were the first works to be published under the name 'Shakespeare' and for the next five years the records show the byline 'Shakespeare' to have been associated exclusively with these two poems. Plays under the name 'Shakespeare' did not appear in print until 1598, the year that Lord Burghley died.

In May 1577 Oxford invested in Frobisher's voyage in the ship *Edward Bonaventure*. Despite its name, the ship's voyage across the Atlantic in search of the North-West Passage lost money; consequently he was forced to sell three estates (cf. Hamlet's words 'I am but mad north-north-west' II.1.). In 1578 he invested in Frobisher's second expedition, which also lost money, forcing further sales of estates.

He was mentioned by Gabriel Harvey in an address to Queen Elizabeth in July 1578, as a prolific private poet and one 'whose countenance shakes spears'. In the same year John Lyly, Oxford's secretary, published *Euphues. The Anatomy of Wit*, followed in 1579 by *Euphues and his England*, dedicated to Oxford. These two books launched the fashion for 'Euphuism', a style characterized by high-flown language, satirized in *Love's Labour's Lost*.

In March 1581 Oxford's mistress, Anne Vavasour, who was one of Queen Elizabeth's Ladies of the Bedchamber, gave birth to a son. The lovers and their son were sent to the Tower by an infuriated Queen but swiftly released (cf. *Measure for Measure*). After his release, Oxford was wounded in a street-fight provoked by Thomas Knyvet, a kinsman of Anne Vavasour; affrays continued in the streets of London between the rival gangs of supporters for over a year (cf.*Romeo and Juliet*).

In December 1581 he resumed living with his long-suffering and devoted wife, and accepted Elizabeth

Vere as his child. Tragically, their only son died one day after his birth. Three more daughters followed, of whom Susan and Bridget survived.

In 1584, Robert Greene's *Gwydonius; the Card of Fancy* was dedicated to him, identifying him as a 'pre-eminent writer'. In 1586, when he was 36, he served on the tribunal which condemned Mary, Queen of Scots to execution.

In the same year, the Queen awarded Oxford an unconditional pension of £1,000 a year for life (about £500,000 at today's value). The motive for this uncharacteristic generosity on the part of the Queen remains a mystery – no accounting was required of Oxford. Her successor, King James I, continued to pay the pension. In reply to Sir Robert Cecil's request that Lord Sheffield's pension be increased, the King refused, saying, 'Great Oxford got no more . . .', leaving us to wonder why Great Oxford? His greatness does not seem to have resided in war or any of the known offices of State. Perhaps a clue can be found in a letter to Burghley, written in 1594, in which Edward de Vere seeks his favour in a matter involving what he describes as 'in mine office' and that this office is beholden to the Queen.

In 1589, George Puttenham published *The Arte of English Poesie* and this contains the most telling recognition of Edward de Vere's literary standing amongst his contemporaries: 'And in her Majesties time that now is are sprong up an other crew of Courtly makers Noble men and Gentlemen of her Majesties owne servantes, who have written excellently well as it would appeare if their doings could be found out and made publicke with the rest, of which number is first that noble Gentleman Edward Earle of Oxford.'

In 1588 his wife Anne, daughter of Lord Burghley, died and in extant letters written at this time, it is reported that Burghley is so incapacitated by grief over the death of his favourite daughter that he is incapable of conducting any Privy Council business.

Three years later, in 1591, Oxford married another of the Queen's Maids of Honour, Elizabeth Trentham, with whom he finally became the father of a male heir; Henry de Vere, 18th Earl of Oxford. Although there is evidence of his continued involvement in Court affairs, from the date of this marriage Edward de Vere's life at his new home at King's Place in Hackney is perhaps the most obscure of his entire life.

In 1594, his ship the *Edward Bonaventure* was wrecked in Bermuda (cf. *The Tempest*). In January 1595, Elizabeth Vere married William Stanley, 6th Earl of Derby, another literary earl who maintained his own company of players – many scholars believe that *A Midsummer Night's Dream* was written for these festivities which were attended by the whole royal Court.

On September 7 1598, Francis Meres' *Palladis Tamia* was registered for publication, naming Oxford as the 'best for comedy'. This is a vital document in Shakespearean history because it includes the first mention of 'Shakespeare' as a playwright, attributing twelve plays to him; until then Shakespeare's reputation had rested on the two narrative poems only.

Oxford suffered all his life from financial difficulties, much of which can be traced to the fact that Queen Elizabeth handed out the bulk of his estate to her favourite courtier the Earl of Leicester during Oxford's minority as a royal ward (estates which Oxford found almost impossible to reclaim), and the ruinous debt she placed upon him over his marriage to Anne Cecil. It is, however, notable that his new brother-in-law, the wealthy Staffordshire landowner and Knight of the Shire Francis Trentham, took over the management of Edward de

Vere's near-bankrupt estate from 1591 and gradually nursed it back to health so that, when Oxford died, all of his massive debts had been cleared.

On the Queen's death in 1603 Oxford wrote eloquently to Sir Robert Cecil, son and heir of Lord Burghley, of his 'great grief'. He wrote, 'In this common shipwreck, mine is above all the rest, who least regarded, though often comforted, she hath left to try my fortune among the alterations of time and chance'.

Oxford died in Hackney in 1604, cause unknown. Parish records state that he was buried in Hackney Church on July 6, but a family history by his first cousin Percival Golding, states 'Edward de Veer … a man in mind and body absolutely accomplished with honorable endowments … lieth buried at Westminster'. No record of such a burial can now be traced in Westminster Abbey, where there is a Vere family tomb.

The Aftermath of Oxford's life and death

During the winter season 1604-05, six of Shakespeare's plays were presented at Court by command of King James I. This has an air of commemoration. In 1609 the *Sonnets* were published in a pirated edition. The famous dedication describes the author as 'our ever-living', a phrase invariably used only of the dead.

In 1622 Henry Peacham published, in *The Compleat Gentelman*, a list of poets who made Elizabeth's reign a 'golden age'. Unaccountably, he omitted Shakespeare but placed the Earl of Oxford in first place in his list – perhaps he knew them to be the same person. This is unlike Meres who included them both – maybe one reason was because he didn't know Oxford and Shakespeare were the same person.

127

We do not know who instigated publication of the First Folio Edition of the Shakespeare plays in 1623, but there is no mention of any executor or relative of Shakspere of Stratford in connection with it. However, of the two brothers who financed it and to whom it was dedicated, one – Philip Earl of Montgomery – was the husband of Oxford's daughter Susan, while the other – William Earl of Pembroke – had once been a suitor for her sister Bridget. Pembroke was Lord Chamberlain, the supreme authority in the world of theatre, and thus in a position to decide which plays were to be published and which suppressed. We also know that Ben Jonson, who wrote much of the introductory material, was an intimate associate of the de Vere family after Oxford's death. The First Folio was therefore very much a family affair, but the family was not the one in Stratford-on-Avon.

An AfterVerse

For those with yet an interest
In strenuous debate
We've compiled a list of books and films
Your appetite to sate.
From this study clear your mind
Of doubt and all misgiving-
Who from us has long since gone
And who is ever-living.

Selected References & Bibliography
About the Author
Edward de Vere, 17th Earl of Oxford

Books

♦ Anderson, M. (2005). *Shakespeare by Another Name: The Life of Edward de Vere, Earl of Oxford, The Man who was Shakespeare.* New York: Gotham Books. *--A physicist by training with research interest in how evidence supports or negates a theory, Mark Anderson spent ten years investigating Edward de Vere as the author of Shake-speare's works.*

♦Farina, William. (2006). *De Vere as Shakespeare: An Oxfordian Reading of the Canon.* Jefferson, NC. McFarland & Company.

--Each of the plays and poems is individually assessed and explored in its own chapter, using the innumerable connections between the text itself and the life of its author, Edward de Vere.

♦ Looney, J. Thomas (2018). *Shakespeare Identified.* Cary, N.C. Veritas Publicaations.
--First published in 1920 this book began the modern Oxfordian movement. From reading it, Sigmund Freud became convinced and John Galsworthy called it "the best detective story I ever read."

♦ Ogburn, C. (1992). *The Mysterious William Shakespeare.* McLean (Va.): EPM.
--An in depth exploration and must read foundational book on the authorship question.

♦Sobran, Joseph. (1997). *Alias Shakespeare: Solving the Greatest Literary Mystery of All Time.*
New York; The Free Press, A Division of Simon & Schuster.
--A concise exploration of the puzzling questions surrounding the authorship controversy with the evidence decisively supporting the case for Edward de Vere, the 17th Earl of Oxford, as the rightful author of the Shakespeare plays and poems.

♦Whittemore, Hank. (2016), *100 Reasons Shake-speare Was the Earl of Oxford.*
Somerville MA. Forever Press.
►Also with further discussion and public comment at: *Hank Whittemore's Shakespeare Blog.*
        https://hankwhittemore.com/
--In both the book and online blog cited above, Whittemore presents a concise introduction to the

authorship question that examines 100 different aspects, from biographical and historical records, that point to Edward de Vere as the true writer of the Shake-speare plays and poems.

Websites & Videos

► De Vere Society. (2019). The de Vere Society – Dedicated to the proposition that the works of Shakespeare were written by Edward de Vere, 17th Earl of Oxford. [online] Deveresociety.co.uk. Available at: https://deveresociety.co.uk
--A very complete resource with substantial biographical and authorship information and links.

► The Oxford Fellowship (2019). Shakespeare Oxford Fellowship | Research and Discussion of the Shakespeare Authorship Question. [online] Shakespeare Oxford Fellowship. Available at: https://shakespeareoxfordfellowship.org/
--A seminal online resource especially focusing on the authorship question.

► Waugh, A. (2019). Alexander Waugh. [online] YouTube. Available at: https://www.youtube.com/channel/UCHN7SCKlsa9lPYJ mqqQ2uIg/featured/
OR simply search: 'Alexander Waugh'
--Alexander Waugh is a leading authorship scholar who has produced many fascinating video presentations on the authorship question. This link is to his YouTube Channel.

► Columbia Pictures & Centropolis Entertainment. (2011). *Anonymous.* Produced and directed by Roland Emmerich. [DVD]

--This mainstream film is both entertaining and enlightening. It presents a superb dramatization of the character of Edward de Vere, setting out in detail the historical and personal context which made his anonymous authorship necessary.

► Centropolis Entertainment and First Folio Pictures. *Last Will and Testament.* (2012). [DVD]
--A thoughtful and ground-breaking video documentary introduction to the Shakespeare authorship question.

Acknowledgment

Our sincere thanks to
The de Vere Society
and
The Shakespeare Oxford Fellowship
*for their inspiration, help and support
in creating this series.*

Attributions

*--Character list from Wikipedia under
the Creative Commons License 3.0
--Play text from the Moby(tm) editions
in the public domain*

Photos

Coat of Arms of Edward de Vere
Source: Wikimedia.org
Author: George Baker / Public domain

The Keep at Castle Hedingham
Source: geograph.org.uk
Author: David Phillips / CC BY-SA 2.0

The de Vere Family Coat of Arms
Source: Wikimedia
Author: Rs-nourse / CC BY-SA 3.0
(https://creativecommons.org/licenses/by-sa/3.0)

View from The Minstrels' Gallery, Hedingham Castle
Source: geograph.org.uk/p/3162585
Photo by: © PAUL FARMER - cc-by-sa/2.0

Cover/Inside: The Welbeck portrait of Edward de Vere (1575). Artist unknown. National Portrait Gallery, London.

This work has been edited and produced by

Verus Publishing

www.verusbooks.com

V | P

www.ingramcontent.com/pod-product-compliance
Lightning Source LLC
Chambersburg PA
CBHW030418100426
42812CB00028B/3015/J